BETWEEN MIDNIGHT AND DAY

THE LAST UNPUBLISHED BLUES ARCHIVE

Between Midnight and Day,
The Last Unpublished Blues Archive.
©2003 by Dick Waterman

Published by

THUNDER'S
MOUTH
PRESS

Thunder's Mouth Press
An Imprint of Avalon Publishing Group
245 West 17th street, 11th floor
New York, NY 10011-5300
Distributed by Publishers Group West

Produced by

INSIGHT EDITIONS

17 Paul Drive
San Rafael, CA 94903
www.insighteditions.com

Library of Congress
Cataloging-in-Publication Data

Waterman, Dick.
Between Midnight and Day:
The Last Unpublished Blues Archive
By Dick Waterman;
Introduction ©Peter Guralnick;
Preface ©Bonnie Raitt.

p.cm.

ISBN: 1-56025-547-1

1. Blues (Music)—History and criticism.
2. Blues musicians. I. Title.

ML3521.W39 2003
781.643'09--dc21

2003055958

9 8 7 6 5 4 3 2 1

Cover and layout design by Palace Press International
Printed in China by Palace Press International
Distributed by Publishers Group West

This book is published in conjunction with
the exhibition:
Between Midnight and Day,
The Photographs of Dick Waterman

Govinda Gallery
1227 34th St. NW
Washington DC 20007
www.govindagallery.com

BETWEEN MIDNIGHT AND DAY

THE LAST UNPUBLISHED BLUES ARCHIVE

DICK WATERMAN

THUNDER'S
MOUTH
PRESS

To lovers of the *blues*...

Buddy Guy, 1968

Table of *Contents*

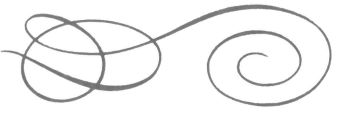

During the winter of 1996, my thirteen-year-old son, David, said to me, "Why don't we go trace the roots of the blues?" David had been listening to a lot of blues records, including the recordings of Son House, Robert Johnson, Charley Patton, and Blind Lemon Jefferson. He had also been reading Francis Davis's book, *The History of the Blues.*

Inspired by David's suggestion, I replied, "Let's do it," and we found ourselves a few weeks later at the Riverside Hotel in Clarksdale, Mississippi, sitting with its proprietor, Mrs. Z. L. Hill. The Riverside is known to be, among other things, the place where Bessie Smith died in 1937 following an automobile accident on Highway 61. Mrs. Hill enjoyed David and his precocious love of the blues, and she showed him the room where Bessie Smith had passed away. We visited the cabin where Muddy Waters lived on the Stovall Farm plantation. I enjoyed a shave at Wade Walton's barber shop while David played guitar with Walton himself (the bluesman formerly of Ike Turner's *Kings of Rhythm*). We sought out the legendary "crossroads" sung about by Robert Johnson, where it is

FOREWORD

CHRIS MURRAY

and exhibiting significant photographs related to music, I was very curious about these singular, previously unseen images. I noticed that the subjects of the exhibition were not second or third generation blues musicians, and the photographs were not taken during the 1980s or 1990s. Most of them dated from the first so-called blues revival, which took place during the mid-1960s. The vintage of these photographs only added to the intimacy of the images. There were portraits of every blues legend that I knew, and then some—names like Son House, Skip James, Furry Louis, Mississippi John Hurt, Will Shade, Muddy Waters, Sippie Wallace, Willie Dixon, Albert King, Otis Rush, the Reverend Gary Davis, and many more.

In my experience as curator of photographic exhibitions and my work with the individuals that took the photographs, I had come to learn that *access* was key. The photographer who took these blues photos certainly had access. Although the collection was modestly presented—rather simple, eleven-by-fourteen inch black and white photos—I was knocked out by what I saw. I asked for the photographer's name and left my

said Johnson sold his soul to the devil in exchange for mastery of the guitar.

We then drove east to Oxford, Mississippi. A brief story about Oxford in the *Washington Post* convinced me that it was well worth a visit. After checking in at a local guest house, we walked to the town's center. On the way, I happened to look in the window of a small frame shop, and inside were the most compelling photographs of blues musicians I had ever seen. I went in and enjoyed a small exhibition of these photographs, none of which I had seen before. As someone who, at that time, had spent more than a dozen years researching

card and a local phone number. A few hours later, I was on the phone with the man who took these classic blues photographs, Dick Waterman. That same evening, my son David and I, along with my girlfriend Carlotta Hester, were eating dinner with Waterman at a restaurant on the Oxford town square. That meeting turned into the beginning of a friendship that would reveal to me the world of the blues as I had never known before. Inspired by his photographs and extraordinary firsthand accounts of the blues legends, I told Waterman that I would like to organize an exhibition of his images and help him publish a book of them along with his stories. I could see that Waterman's photographs and stories constituted a uniquely important visual document and oral history of the blues.

This book presents, for the first time, many of Waterman's most significant photographs from his blues archive. There is an immediacy to these pictures...there is no artifice. Seen along with Waterman's stories, the reader has a sense of "being there"—of feeling the intense heat in the stark portrait of Will Shade on a Memphis evening in 1964; of hearing the sublimely elegant guitar and voice in the transcendent image of B.B. King in Newport in 1968; of seeing the genuine camaraderie and love between close friends in the photographs of Buddy Guy and Junior Wells taken in Ann Arbor in 1969. One can understand the grace and soul of an artist like Son House after seeing Waterman's extraordinary portrait taken at the Liberty Bell in 1965. One can know the yearning in Robert Pete Williams's heart for his beloved wife, Hattie Mae, as he sits alone at the bottom of a stairway and sings softly to her in Waterman's intimate and tender photograph taken in Philadelphia in 1969.

Perhaps the most compelling result of Waterman's work is that we also have access to these blues legends. We are fortunate to share in the spirit of these great songwriters and musicians through the artistry of Dick Waterman.

Bonnie Raitt and Junior Wells

P R E F A C E

As a love-struck blues fan and freshman at Harvard in 1968, I used to sit glued to the WHRB radio station blues shows. One afternoon, my classmate asked if I might want to meet Son House, who was going to be at Dick Waterman's house after his radio show. That afternoon changed my life. My friendship with Dick developed as closely as did those with the many blues artists we both adored. Through his connection I received the education and gift of a lifetime—hanging and learning about life and music from all my heroes as well as being given a job I'd love for the rest of my life. Within a couple of years, I was opening for his acts and Dick went on to manage me for the next fifteen years.

While so many mostly white, middle class blues aficionados seem to obsess about only the actual Blues recordings, huddling around their hallowed '78s, speaking in hushed tones about this or that obscure song, the living, breathing scions of the music walk among us. Often forgotten, neglected, and long occupied

B O N N I E   R A I T T

in jobs other than music—farmer, porter, you name it—having given up on the idea of recognition or making a living in music, they suddenly found their lives transformed by being 'rediscovered' during the heralded Folk/Blues revival of the mid-1960s.

After starting his own management and booking agency, Avalon Productions, Dick knew the meaning of rent money, medical bills, proper billing and payment; how to get a person from some small town in the Delta up to the big East Coast cities for gigs and back. He knew how to help these often rural, unsophisticated geniuses fare in the alien, impossibly whirlwind world of the folk/blues festival and concert circuit.

By gathering so many greats under one roof, Dick was able to collectively bargain to insure each artist got to play the best gigs and be paid what they deserved. He steadfastly guarded every aspect of his artists' professional life and was often their families solid rock during personal crises as well. By helping to raise the quality of life for so many artists with whom he worked, by reminding the white progeny of these mighty scions wherein their debt lies, by refusing to compromise probably at the expense of his own advancement, and by taking the high road and loving the people as well as the music, Dick has helped shepherd the Blues to a place in history truly befitting its worth.

For this, and for the gift that are these extraordinary images and reminiscences brought together in this book, we thank you.

SON HOUSE HOLDING A NATIONAL

I'm not sure when exactly I met Dick for the first time. My friends and I had all fallen in love with the blues at an early age, and it seemed as if every time we stood in line to see one of our heroes, Dick was on the inside with the people who actually knew them. When we first went to see Mississippi John Hurt at a little coffeehouse in the shadow of Fenway Park in early 1964, Dick was promoting the show. When the legendary Delta blues singer, Son House, who had not been heard from since 1942, made his first public appearance a few months later after being tracked down in Rochester, New York by Dick, Phil Spiro, and Nick Perls, Dick was standing right by his side as he incongruously took the stage among a procession of city-bred folk singers at Club 47's regular Sunday night hootenanny. At Newport, when Skip James, also rediscovered that same spring, sang the first haunting notes of his 1931 classic, "Devil Got My Woman," Dick captured the moment with the dramatically framed photograph that you will see on page 25.

It was through another of those rediscovered blues singers that I first ran afoul of Dick, if only for a very brief time. I had just learned of the existence of the English magazine, *Blues Unlimited*, and begun corresponding with its editors without ever having seen an issue of the magazine itself. It was exciting to find fellow enthusiasts, and with the bravado of the letter-writer who never imagines that he might some day be held accountable for his words, I offered up free-wheeling opinions and unfiltered accounts of what was happening on the local blues scene. What was my surprise, then, when Dick walked up to me at Club 47 and said, "I ought to punch you in the face." It might have

been one of the first times I had ever gotten anything more elaborate than a courteous greeting from him, and I was genuinely perplexed. "Did you write this?" he said, waving an issue of the British blues magazine in front of me and forcing me to read my own unguarded words about the physical appearance and manner of one of the blues singers he was managing. There wasn't anything to do but stammer an apology as I was made to confront my own supercilious attitude. Dick might just as well have said to me, "Don't be such a smart-ass. Only a jerk shows off at the expense of others." And it didn't really make me feel all that much better when, some time later, after he was no longer representing the singer, Dick admitted that he might have shared some of my aesthetic reservations. It wasn't the criticism, it was the self-serving tone that he was objecting to, a lesson I have tried to keep in mind ever since.

In every other regard Dick was not only forbearing, he extended himself in ways that far surpassed anything that one had any right to expect—so long as you adhered to his code of playing fair. When I called to set up an interview with Skip James, the very first interview I had ever even contemplated doing (and one on which I was prepared to embark only because I *was* convinced that greatness such as this would not pass my way again), my voice, I'm sure, was trembling as I tried to convince first myself, and then Dick, that this could be an important step in focusing attention on a neglected American genius. But Dick just brushed aside my rationalizations and graciously accepted me on my own terms. For no better reason, I like to think, than his recognition that deep down I really *was* sincere. Which was, and remains, his one abiding gauge for doing business.

PETER GURALNICK

I saw this quality in Dick again and again through the years. Some time after Club 47 closed in 1968, when there were no more blues clubs left in town, a bunch of us started the Boston Blues Society, which, through its affiliation with the Harvard radio station, was able to put on a series of concerts at various university locations over the next couple of years. There were probably eight or ten of us at one time or another, and we brought in Son House, Johnny Shines, Fred McDowell, Houston Stackhouse, Robert Pete Williams, and Otis Rush, among others—but we couldn't have done any of it without Dick, who by this time was managing Bonnie Raitt as well as his usual stable of blues acts and who was our conduit to the greater world. He patiently monitored, mentored, and mid-wifed the shows, persuaded the artists that they were not going to be let down or financially exploited by our inexperience, and generally gave us an education in the music business, until the clubs started springing up again and we could let go of our brief foray into concert promotion.

This was around the same time that I started work on my first book, *Feel Like Going Home*, and once again Dick provided an invaluable service, overcoming any number of obstacles of communication and geography to help me set up an interview with Robert Pete Williams in rural Louisiana, and generously (*very* generously, for there was never any thought of recompense) providing me with some of the book's most striking photographs. Dick himself was just leaving Cambridge at the time, and rather than wait until he was resettled and could make additional prints, he just pushed whatever pictures he had on hand at me. "Here, you take them," he said, insisting that he knew I would take good care of them.

That is the kind of impulsive act of generosity that is typical of Dick but that unfortunately has not always worked to his advantage. In this case it did. Through a series of relocations, flooded cellars, and friends who went through similar life experiences, the negatives for a number of the pictures were lost. And in the end the only original prints of a few (including the one of Skip James raising his unearthly falsetto to the heavens) were the ones he had given me, to help make my book better, on that long-ago spring day.

Dick's much better organized today—well, maybe not all *that* much. He's no less generous, though, and that same sense of decency, honor, puzzled quizzicality, and determined eccentricity still prevails. Not to mention his obsession with keeping the historical record straight. Anyone who's ever heard Dick tell his wonderful stories knows how important not just the photographs but the people, and not just the people but the worlds that they inhabit, are to him. As a manager Dick committed himself long ago to the eternal quest for justice, but as a photographer he committed himself to something no less quixotic: the view beyond the horizon. It's like those songs that Robert Pete Williams plucked out of the air. At their best they communicate something that is at once both intimate and distant, much as Dick's photographs and recollections of Son House, Skip James, Mississippi John Hurt, Howlin' Wolf on the *Shindig* set, Robert Pete Williams in the stairwell of Dick's apartment building all suggest a passion for exploration. They are not about a frozen past. Instead, they provoke a yearning to see what's just around the corner.

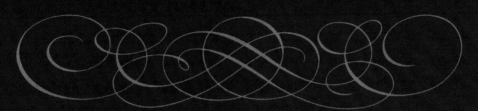

Above

SKIP JAMES, NEWPORT FOLK FESTIVAL, 1965

Following

SON HOUSE, NEWPORT BEACH, CA, 1965

THE ARTISTS

Philadelphia, 1964

For someone who comes from outside of the world of blues music, there has to be a point of entry from which to explore. For some, it might have been the Rolling Stones doing a Robert Johnson song, Canned Heat recording with John Lee Hooker, or perhaps Bonnie Raitt helping to popularize Sippie Wallace.

For me, it was meeting Mississippi John Hurt.

When he first came onstage at the 1963 Newport Folk Festival, I had already seen Josh White, Brownie McGhee and Sonny Terry, and other blues artists. But Mississippi John was something else altogether. He was a small man, seemingly lost amid the affluent white society so far from his home on a Mississippi farm. He carried himself with a special sense of dignity and quiet country wisdom.

One evening, John was booked to play at the Gaslite, a small Greenwich Village coffeehouse. Before the gig, I took him to see *Hard Day's Night* and *Help* at an afternoon matinee double-feature. He got all of the jokes and laughed at all the right times. Later, at the Gaslite, he was having trouble bringing his guitar into tune. As he hit the string and turned the peg gently, John said to the audience, "Me and Dick went to the moving picture show this afternoon."

I was standing in the narrow aisle by the side of the stage, plainly within view of the crowd. I had a bad feeling about where this was going.

"What did you see?" someone called out.

John finished tuning and sat up in his chair. He cocked his head and turned toward me. "I don't rightly recall but it was the same boys in both of them movies. Dick, what was the name of them boys?"

I felt hundreds of eyes turn toward me. It was 1965, the time of acoustic versus amplified, folk versus rock, innocence versus pagan lust. "Uhmmm," I muttered, looking into the darkness and then back to John, bathed in the stage lighting. "It was The Beatles."

The silence was palpable and then the voice of doom came from the darkness. "You took Mississippi John Hurt to see The Beatles?"

John brightened at the name. "Them boys was good," he declared. "You should have seen them jumping and playing them guitars when they was in the snow."

He had saved me from being pilloried throughout folk music eternity.

In between sets at the Gaslite, we did our drinking between sets upstairs at a bar called The Kettle of Fish. There was a young waiter named Tommy who loved John and always made sure that he was taken care of immediately. One night we were drinking when Tommy came by the table and told us that it was his last night. His family owned a funeral home in Rhode Island, so he was going home to learn how to embalm in order to take over the business.

As we finished our drinks and headed for the door, Tommy called out, "Good-bye, John. I hope I see you again some time."

John turned and smiled at Tommy. "Yeah, but I hope it ain't any time soon."

MISSISSIPPI

J O H N   H U R T

One of the last shows I did with John was at the Caffè Lena in Saratoga Springs, New York. We were in the dressing room packing up after the show when a young man said, "When will I get to see you again, John?"

The small man folded the towel over his guitar and closed the case. He looked at the young man and said, "Well, now, you can see me any time you want."

"Really?" the young man replied. "I mean, when are you coming back here?"

John nodded toward me and said, "You'll have to talk to Dick about the booking thing, but you can see me any time that you want." The room was quiet as John touched the fingers of his right hand to his heart. "You see, now that I have met you, I have taken you down into my heart as my friend.

"And I hope that if I am your friend, that you have me in your heart. So any time you want me to be with you, all you have to do is think of me and I'll come right up out of your heart.

"If you have taken me to be your friend, I will always be with you because good friends live forever in your heart."

Previous

MISSISSIPPI JOHN HURT, CAFÉ YANA, BOSTON, 1964   *I promoted a sold-out week of shows for John at the Café Yana in Boston, a small folk club located at the bridge between Fenway Park and Kenmore Square. We were fortunate to have mild weather even though it was the middle of February. It was an incredible joy to hear him play every night for a week.*

After I had closed up the box office for the late show on his last night, I took my camera and moved close to the stage. I crouched down, opened the camera lens wide and slowly began to take pictures. There was only one light overhead and I moved the shutter speed down from 1/60 to 1/30, then down to 1/15, to 1/8, and finally to 1/4. This photograph has remained my personal favorite of all the thousands that I have taken. Mississippi John is serene in the light, an image floating in the darkness.

Opposite

MISSISSIPPI JOHN HURT, PHILADELPHIA, 1964

Opposite

MISSISSIPPI JOHN HURT, TRAIN STATION, CINCINNATI, 1966

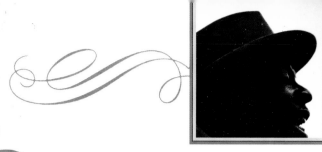
Newport Folk Festival, 1964

Skip James is probably the blues world's finest example of unrealized potential. A huge opportunity was presented to him, but Skip's career languished and he remained underappreciated during his lifetime.

He was last known by audiences when he recorded for Paramount Records in 1931, and then he vanished for over three decades. In June of 1964, he was in a Tunica, Mississippi, hospital when he was found and brought north to recuperate in Washington, D.C. A few weeks later, Skip was brought to the Newport Folk Festival. Blues aficionados were eager to hear this mysterious individual with the high quavering voice whose few recordings brought forth more questions than they answered.

The "Performer" badges had all been distributed by the time Skip arrived at the festival grounds, so he wore a "Kin" badge intended for the relatives of the performers. Before going on stage, he tuned his borrowed guitar under the watchful eye of Mississippi John Hurt, a veteran blues man who had made his own sensational rediscovery appearance the previous year at that same Newport festival.

When Skip was introduced, he sat motionless for an instant and then took a deep breath and tipped his head back, silhouetting himself against a gray summer sky. I have rarely had any photographic sense of capturing a grand historic moment, but I knew that I wanted this moment…this song…this word…this very first note of Skip James's rediscovery caught on film.

His voice was clear and riveting. "I'd rather be the devil," he sang, "than to be that woman's man."

Skip only knew three or four songs at that point, but he delivered them with a passion and authenticity beyond anyone's expectation. He received a standing ovation and the word swept across the festival grounds that the newly rediscovered Skip James had delivered a stunning performance. They found 15 minutes of stage time for him at the evening concert and he repeated the same songs, only this time to 15,000 people, all of whom were mesmerized by his performance. One of the greatest Mississippi blues artists of all time had stepped out of the shadows and cleared away any speculation as to his whereabouts.

Skip James was back.

The only problem was that his handlers didn't know what to do with the opportunity that had been given to them. He could have had a recording contract immediately, gone into the studio, and released an album that would have brought him the visibility needed to book colleges and festivals. Instead, he traveled around as Mississippi John Hurt's opening act, making little money, and squandering the chance to use his Newport triumph as a launching point for further success.

A full year had passed when he returned to Newport for the 1965 festival. By then, the buzz had vanished and he was just another talented blues artist looking for a record deal. While standing by the side of the blues stage, I was approached by someone who said that Skip James wanted to talk to me. I was curious to know what he wanted since we had only nodded hello to each other a few times over the past year.

He waited until I sat down and he offered his hand. "My name is Skip James and you are Dick Waterman."

Above

I nodded my head as he lit a Viceroy cigarette and turned towards me. "Now I know that you doing the business for Son House and I see how he plays lots of festivals and he got himself a record out on Columbia.

"Now the boys doing Skip's business are nice boys but that's what they are. They are boys. Now Skip, he needs a man to do his business, so I figured that I should get the man who is Son House's man."

After talking for a little while, we shook hands. I managed his career for the few years that he had left before he died of cancer. During that time, I did my best but he didn't have enough leverage to get a strong record deal. He had squandered that charismatic wave of renewed popularity that he rode so briefly. I often wondered what I could have done for Skip if I had been involved with him right from the start of his rediscovery.

🎵 *Previous*
Mississippi John Hurt and Skip James, Newport Folk Festival, 1964

Opposite 🎵
Skip James, Newport Folk Festival, 1964

"Skip has come and gone from places that you will never get to."

*S*kip didn't own a guitar of his own, so the Newport Folk Foundation decided to buy him one. He came up to New York City from his home in Philadelphia and went to the Folkore Center on Sixth Avenue. At the Center, they took guitars down from the walls and brought others out of cases and back store rooms. Skip played one after another, discarding some immediately, and holding on to others for a second and third trial.

As the word swept through Greenwich Village that the great Skip James was sitting in the Folklore Center playing guitars, blues fans raced to the scene. He played for hours until finally, he narrowed his choice down to a Yamaha and a big bodied Martin. Unable to decide, he played one and then the other, shaking his head. He picked up the Martin and turned to the store manager.

"Where is this guitar from?" he asked.

"It's made in Nazareth, Pennsylvania."

Skip picked up the Yamaha and played a delicate filigree of notes. "Where is this guitar from?"

"That guitar is from Japan."

Skip nodded his head slowly and looked from one guitar to the other. The guitarists in the room were astounded by what they were seeing. In the context of the mid-1960s, Japan was known only for imitating the better products from other countries–the "Japanese knockoffs" of automobiles, photography gear, and home stereo equipment were considered very inferior. To think that Skip James considered a Yamaha guitar to be the equal of an exalted Martin was boggling. Skip sat motionless for several seconds and then pointed to the Martin.

"Now if anything come up wrong with this guitar, I can just take it up to that town in Pennsylvania where it come from and they'll fix it, right?"

The manager nodded his head. Yes, the Martin company would repair it for him.

Skip nodded toward the Yamaha. "But now this here guitar, I would have to send it all the way back to Japan if it needed to be fixed."

No one really knew. Yamaha had not been in business in America long enough for anyone to have an answer. Skip picked up the Martin and played a few notes.

"I'll take this one. At least I know where I can take it in case something come up wrong."

Yamaha never knew how close they came to having their fledgling first steps into the American guitar market bolstered by one of the most discriminating guitarists of all times.

Skip, having more than his share of vanity, reveled when a fan rained compliments upon him. He would listen with great interest, nodding his head at particularly lavish offerings. But he could be curt when his privacy was invaded. One night at a club a young man walked into a small dressing room uninvited and committed a cardinal sin against any professional musician: he took Skip's guitar out of its case and began to play one of Skip's songs. The young man played with little talent but great enthusiasm. At the end of the song, he smiled at Skip, "Hey, man, do I have you down or do I have you down?"
Skip took the guitar from him and put it back in the case. Then he turned and spoke without emotion, "Skip has come and gone from places that you will never get to."

THE LAST UNPUBLISHED **3** BLUES ARCHIVE
                                          1

SON HOUSE

I did a lot of things wrong in the music business but my appreciation *of Son House was not one of them. Right from the first day that I helped rediscover him, I knew that I had been entrusted with the responsibility of shepherding one of the most powerful performing artists of all time to his audience.

Son was so many paradoxes rolled into one. He was soft-spoken and modest, yet his music was aggressive and commanding. He told self-deprecating stories, but his aura was compelling to behold. I have always said that you could measure the true greatness of Son House not by watching him, but by looking at Muddy Waters, Howling Wolf, or Jimmy Reed as *they* watched him.

Son carried himself with the grace of a true survivor. He went through more than his share of battles and emerged with a tranquility that surrounded him, except when he began to play his music. He would sit far back in his chair and speak so softly that his words were almost inaudible. Then he would sit up and put his left hand down the neck of the guitar, laying his slide against the strings. After pausing momentarily to take a breath, Son would suddenly rip the slide up the strings and the sound of the steel body National would resound to the farthest corners of the room, while his low and throaty voice would suddenly soar into impassioned falsetto.

The songs would last sometimes six, sometimes ten minutes; he would go on and on until his story had been told. Eyes shut tight and sweat dripping down his face, Son House would transport himself to another time and place. He might go back to 1928 or 1938...he might be back in Robinsonville or Clarksdale or to towns in his far distant past.

When the song ended, Son would slump forward for a few seconds and then slowly raise his head. He would blink his eyes, refocusing on the present. Chuckling softly as he slid back in the chair, he would begin to tell another story. Only songs about the travails of human frailty interested him. "Ain't no kind of blues excepting between a man and a woman," he would say, nodding solemnly.

There's an old expression that says little dogs play in the middle of the street until the big dog comes down off of the porch and the little dogs run away.

Son House was the "big dog" of the blues world.

In 1941 and 1942, Son had been recorded in Mississippi by Alan Lomax for the Library of Congress. Then Son vanished completely for over two decades until he was found in Rochester, New York, in 1964. When Son and I walked onto the Newport Folk Festival grounds in July of that year, I spotted Lomax walking toward us.

Son saw him coming and remarked, "Here come that old booger Lomax."

Before I had a chance to respond, Lomax was upon us and shaking hands with Son. "How are you, Son? Still living by the bridge in Rochester?"

Stunned that Lomax knew where Son had been all those lost years, I said, "You knew where Son has been since the 1940s?"

Lomax nodded his head. "Oh, yes, Son and I have stayed in touch over the years, haven't we, Son?"

Wait a goddamn minute. What the hell is going on here? I looked at Lomax, then at Son, and then back to Lomax.

"You knew where one of the greatest blues singers of all time was for over 20 years and never told anyone? Didn't you think it was important to record him and give him a chance to make some money?"

Lomax shrugged his shoulders and replied, "After I recorded him, it wasn't any of my business what he did with his life. My job was to record him for the Library of Congress. I didn't care what he did after that."

As he walked away, I stood there and stared at him for a moment. I wasn't sure if he was ignorant or evil not to have shared the details of Son's whereabouts.

Son turned to me and said, "He come down and recorded me and Willie Brown back then and he didn't give us but one Coca-Cola. Willie grabbed up the Coca-Cola first and I didn't get nothing."

After he resumed playing in 1964, Son House had the usual offers from smaller record labels. I could have settled for that, but I had hopes that he would be signed to a major label.

Remembering that John Hammond had overseen the release of the Robert Johnson album on Columbia, I arranged a meeting to determine if John was interested in producing a Son House record. Son and I were waiting in his office when he came striding through the door, shook our hands quickly, and moved behind his desk.

"I can't tell you what an honor it is to have the great Son House sitting in front of me. Your Paramount sides are some of the greatest recordings of all time. And, of course, Robert Johnson learned so much from you. You know that I tried to bring him to New York City for a concert?"

I glanced at Son and he was looking out the window. This was not a good

Previous

MISSISSIPPI JOHN HURT AND SON HOUSE, PHILADELPHIA, 1964   *Shortly after the rediscoveries of Mississippi John Hurt and Son House in 1963 and 1964, respectively, both were brought to the Philadelphia Folk Festival in August, 1964. Two gifted musicians with very different styles, John and Son had never met before this festival, but they got along right from the beginning. Son has a guitar on his lap, and John's is on the ground beside him.*
I love this photo because it's simply an image of friendship between two men.

Opposite

SON HOUSE, SKIP JAMES, AND MISSISSIPPI JOHN HURT, NEWPORT FOLK FESTIVAL, 1965   *This is the only photo ever taken of the three great blues rediscoveries of the 1960s. Skip James is in the middle with his arms around Son House (left) and Mississippi John Hurt (right). Skip died in 1969, John in 1966, and Son lived on until 1988. They were such different personalities and, as musicians, they found different degrees of success. When I look at this photo, these three faces conjure up an awful lot of memories for me.*

sign. I could tell that his attention was wandering. John, on the other hand, was just getting started. His enthusiasm moved up a notch.

"I was doing the Spirituals to Swing concert back in 1938 and I sent word down south that I wanted Robert to appear on the show but the word came back that he was dead. Can you imagine how great it would have been to have had Robert Johnson on stage at Carnegie Hall?"

Son reached into his shirt pocket and took out a crumpled pack of cigarettes. Crossing one leg over the other, he lit one and looked back out the window. "Uh oh," I thought, "bad sign." I knew from this body language that Son had tuned out on this conversation and had gone into his own world.

John continued with the Robert Johnson superlatives, raving about his incredible talent and what a loss it had been that he died so young. I couldn't get a word in and I didn't want to interrupt, so I just waved my arm in the air until he stopped and looked at me.

"Look, Mister Hammond," I said, "With all due respect to Robert Johnson be-ing a great musician, you have to remember that Son only knows him in the context of being a snotty kid that hung around him and Willie Brown, copping their licks and breaking guitar strings whenever they let him sit in for a few songs.

"He just doesn't have the same appreciation of Robert that you do. Son is a great artist in his own right and it's a little insulting of you to bring us here and then talk about someone else."

I nudged Son with my elbow to get his attention and we both looked up as John quickly moved around the desk and embraced Son. "Welcome to Columbia Records, Son House," he exclaimed. "Welcome to Columbia Records. We are honored to have you here and we are going to make a wonderful record together."

After the meeting, Son and I went downstairs to the bar. I had a beer and ordered a double bourbon on the rocks for him. I lifted my glass and said, "Here's to John Hammond…for bringing you to Columbia Records."

Son held his glass aloft for a moment and said, "Here's to Robert Johnson…for being dead."

Previous

SON HOUSE AND JOHN FAHEY, LOS ANGELES, 1965

Opposite

SON AND EVIE HOUSE, NEWPORT FOLK FESTIVAL, 1966

DICK WATERMAN AND SON HOUSE

Howling Wolf was one tough *son-of-a-bitch.* Don't believe the stories that said he was just a grumpy old man who yelled a lot. He would kick the crap out of you just because it was Tuesday. And then there was the time I introduced Wolf to Bonnie Raitt.

Bonnie was still a college student at Radcliffe at the time, and we drove into New York City to see Wolf play at The Scene, a basement club on West 46th Street just off of Eighth Avenue. He was just finishing his set when we entered the club. He was wearing dark slacks and a white shirt with the sleeves rolled back almost to the elbows.

On his way to the dressing room, Wolf passed through a small alcove that had a flashing strobe light overhead. As he came into the tiny room, the strobe light made his sweat look like melted wax running down his face. He paused when he saw me and shook hands cordially.

"Wolf," I said, "This is my friend Bonnie."

When he looked down at her, that instant was a surreal moment frozen forever in time. He took her small hand inside his huge paw and slowly spoke from the depths of his being.

"Hello, dahhlin'," he whispered.

Wolf released her hand, nodded to me, and moved on to his dressing room. I turned toward Bonnie who was still standing frozen with her hand extended.

"You OK?" I asked.

She turned to me slowly and said, "That is the sexiest man that I have ever met in my life."

In April, 1965, *Son House and I were in California* when we heard that Wolf was doing a Shindig show with the Rolling Stones. We talked our way onto the lot and came onto the set where they were taping. I asked Son, "Are you sure you're going to remember him? You haven't seen him for well over 20 years."

Son nodded. "Oh, yeah, he's a big bag of bones. I'll bet he ain't changed a bit."

We entered the stage from the back and crossed to the front before seeing Wolf sitting alone in a theater seat. He immediately recognized Son and stood up. Wolf emerged from that seat like an elephant coming out of a phone booth. He just unfolded his body in sections until he loomed above us.

Son's eyes got big as he whispered, "Man, he sure has got his growth!"

The two old friends sat and talked at length while the Rolling Stones watched intently. Finally, one of them approached me and asked, "Who's the old man that Wolf is so happy to see?"

"That's Son House," I replied.

The young man nodded his head and said, "Ahh, the one who taught Robert Johnson and Muddy Waters."

Through the years, I have often told the story and have always been asked which one of the Rolling Stones knew immediately who Son House was.

It was Brian Jones.

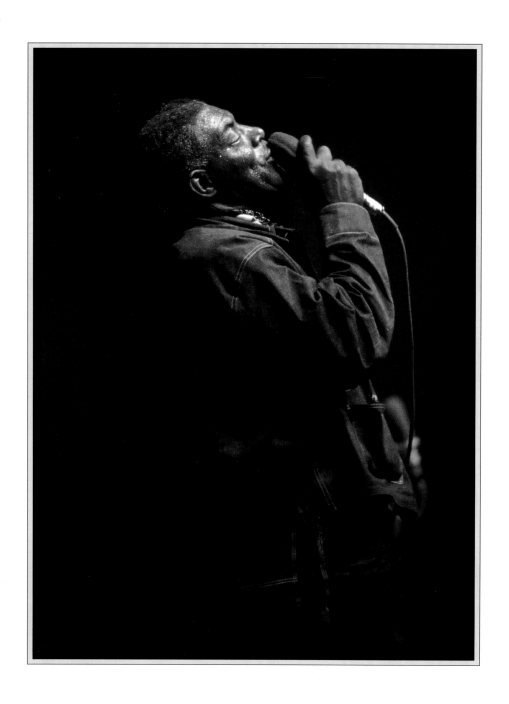

🎵 *Previous*

Son House And Howling Wolf, Los Angeles, Ca, 1965

🎵 *Above*

Howling Wolf, Newport, 1966

During his final years, Wolf, a veteran of World War II, suffered from kidney failure such that his road gigs had to be coordinated with dialysis treatments several times a week in cities with V.A. hospitals. Today this would be a simple matter of cross-referencing on a computer hospital appointments with gigs. Back then it was a tedious and difficult job.

With his left arm bandaged, Wolf would come to the gig after being hooked to a dialysis machine for seven hours. He would begin his performance seated in a chair but, after a few songs, the emotion of his performance would overcome him. He would stand up, toss the chair aside, and prowl the stage, moaning and singing, urging the band to lift him higher. It was a stunning sight to see. Through sheer will, an elderly man who spent hours having his blood cleansed was now sweeping away his illness to bring forth a powerful performance.

Howling Wolf was a force of nature not to be denied.

Newport Folk Festival, 1966

The significance of Muddy Waters in the world of blues music can never be overstated. He took what was essentially a rural form of music and transformed it into the urban art form which continues to influence musicians to the present day.

Shortly after Alan Lomax came through Mississippi in the 1940s doing field records for the Library of Congress, Muddy moved to Chicago, finding himself in a city filled with workers busy in World War II factories. He couldn't play his acoustic music in the noisy clubs, so he added a rhythm section. Eventually, he brought in a piano and a harmonica player and formed what we now consider "Chicago Blues." His early material was still based on southern themes, but it wasn't long before his unique sound made Muddy the star artist on the Chess Records roster.

I had been managing for only a few years when I began adding some Chicago bands to my roster of older acoustic musicians. It was clear that I had to do this or go back to being a newspaperman. I was managing a young band scheduled to open a major concert at a university near the city. My act arrived late and played poorly on borrowed equipment. After the set, I followed the band leader into the dressing room and really tore into him. All of the bands were sharing the same large communal dressing room so all of the other musicians witnessed what was happening.

"When you go up there, all of my artists go up there with you," I said. "Son House goes up. Junior Wells goes up. Your success is our success and your failure is our failure. You screwed up. You weren't ready to play."

As the young man nodded his head in apology and walked away, I turned and saw the eyes of all of the other musicians on me. I had embarrassed a black musician in front of his peers.

I shook my head in futility and started to walk out when I saw someone motion to me. Muddy Waters, wearing a black bandana to cover his "conked" hair, was sitting alone at a long table shuffling a deck of cards. I walked over and sat down next to him. We vaguely knew each other. He was aware of the fact that I managed Son House, his mentor from the Delta. He stopped shuffling and squared off the deck. He looked at me and then, instead of leaning toward me, he sat up straight and put his arm over the back of his chair.

Speaking with his unique cadence, loud enough for the whole room to hear, Muddy said, "Now I heard what you said to the boy…and the boy had it coming to him…boy didn't show no respect for the people… boy didn't come ready to play."

He reached forward to square off the deck of cards and again settled back in his chair. "You done right…you told the boy what he needed to hear…now I been watching you…and you just keep on keeping on like you been doing…and you'll be just fine."

I stood up and walked away, knowing that I wasn't going to be a newspaperman anymore. I could do this management thing.

If I was all right by Muddy Waters, I was going to do just fine.

Previous

MUDDY WATERS, CARNEGIE HALL, NEW YORK, 1965

Opposite

MUDDY WATERS, NEWPORT FOLK FESTIVAL, 1966

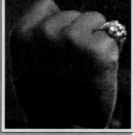

Back around 1967, I used to see B.B. King play at Louie's Lounge, located under the elevated train tracks on Washington Street in the Roxbury section of Boston. I was usually the only white person there, but Louie's was cool and I never felt threatened. After a while B.B. got to know my face and, eventually, my name.

A Eugene McCarthy Presidential rally was held in Fenway Park during the summer of 1968 and I was asked to book talent for it. I approached B. B. and he agreed to play. The capacity of the stadium was 40,000, but it was packed far beyond that number with thousands of people listening on speakers set up in the street. B.B. played his half hour and was packing up his equipment when the word came that McCarthy's motorcade was running late. I told B.B. to go back on and keep playing until McCarthy showed up.

He played for over an hour before the candidate arrived. Showcasing all of his hits that white audiences had not yet heard, B.B. benefited greatly when his performance was followed by McCarthy's stupefyingly dull stump campaign speech. The crowd left buzzing about B.B. King. He was immediately able to cross over into the major rock ballrooms and his appearance prices soared as a result.

A few months later, I was in Philadelphia and went to see B.B. at a bar called Pep's, on the corner of South and Broad streets. The bar consisted of a circular room with the band playing down in a lowered center stage and the tables banked in rows above. I paid my cover charge and went in. While waiting for showtime at a table near the stage, I looked in vain for a waiter. Finally, I realized that the lack of service meant that I probably wasn't entirely welcomed by everyone in the club.

B.B.'s band at the time, "Sonny Freeman and the Unusual," did a few songs before introducing B.B. who opened with a rousing "Every Day I Sing the Blues." As he ended the song, B.B. squinted into the audience, saw one white face, and looked at me.

"Hey, Dick!" he said. "What are you doing here? Nice to see you!"

It started to rain waiters. They were coming at me from all sides as people at adjoining tables offered to send over drinks. I'm not certain what the moral of the story is, but it just shows that knowing B.B. King in Philadelphia makes it real easy to buy a beer.

B. B. KING

Opposite
B.B. KING, NEWPORT FOLK FESTIVAL, 1968

BONNIE RAITT AND B.B. KING, AUSTIN, 1993   *The first weekend in June is "Homecoming Weekend." This is when B.B. returns to Indianola, Mississippi, and plays a concert with a very low ticket price so that everyone can come and see him. B.B. claims that he wants to stay accessible to the poor black people of his hometown, but I really think that the opposite is true. No matter where he goes, what he plays, or how many honors he receives, B.B. King needs to come home to Mississippi to remember where he started and how far his journey has taken him.*

Club 47, Cambridge, 1963

R

everend Gary Davis was managed by Manny Greenhill, not only my mentor but also a man whose wisdom and civility served as guide posts for me during my years as a manager. Since the blues community was so small, rivalries served no purpose and I was always glad to help artists with whom I had no working affiliation.

Such was the case when I traveled to the Mariposa Folk Festival in Toronto one year, and Estelle Klein, the talent booker and promoter, took me aside. "Reverend Davis was just awful last night," she confided. "He had too much to drink and the performance was just terrible. He's scheduled to play again tomorrow night and you've got to help me. I think he really hurt his reputation last night."

I wandered into the dressing room and sat down next to Reverend Davis. Touching him on the wrist, I said, "Reverend, it's Dick Waterman. I understand you had some problems last night."

He shook his head slowly and leaned forward in a conspiratorial manner. "The devil put whiskey before me last night," he whispered, "and I was too weak to leave it be."

Trying to give him confidence, I nodded and said, "Well, you'll have such a good show tomorrow night that no one will even remember what happened. I'll be right here with you." All day Sunday, I stayed with him and kept repeating the same words over and over again. "OK, Reverend, you only have 15 minutes so we're just going to do four songs. We going to go up there, do the four songs, and then come right down."

I helped the Reverend choose the four songs before moving from the dressing room tent to the stage area. There was a set of stairs going up at a very sharp angle to an opening right through the rear of the stage. To make matters worse, there were no hand rails to grip as we went up and down. I waited until the announcer had started his introduction and then I took the Reverend's guitar in my left hand and touched his elbow with my other hand.

"OK, Reverend," I said. "Here we go."

As we slowly climbed the stairs, I could tell that the introduction was going on too long. We were going to arrive at the top of the stairs before he was through, so we continued to climb slowly until suddenly we emerged into the blinding stage lights and moved towards the microphone. The startled announcer jumped aside as I positioned the Reverend and brought his hand to the microphone. Almost all of the blind musicians performed sitting down, but Reverend Davis was one of the few who played standing up. He also had a very slight rocking gait as he played, causing him to drift a tiny bit to the left as the performance moved along.

On this particular night, from the very first song, he started edging to his left, first moving off the microphone and eventually facing to the left side of the stage with his right shoulder toward the audience. I had no choice except to make the correction so I scrambled up behind him and touched his shoulder. "Reverend, you're off the microphone," I said,

REVEREND

GARY DAVIS

taking his right hand and touching it to the microphone again.

His performance was magnificent. He played "Samson and Delilah" better than I had ever heard him do it and followed with a stirring, "If I Had My Way." He finished his four songs and the entire crowd came to their feet. It was a triumph in every way. The Reverend had redeemed himself completely.

With the Reverend leaning on my shoulder, we slowly worked our way down the steep steps in darkness. When we reached the bottom, Estelle Klein was waiting with a question. "Dick," she asked, "Do you think you could take him back up for an encore?"

I looked at her and shook my head. "Estelle," I said, "This would be a very good time to quit while you're ahead."

After his performance, the festival organizers didn't want the Reverend to fly home to LaGuardia Airport alone, so they asked if I would accompany him on my way back to Boston. I agreed to do it and showed up at his hotel room door early the next morning. He had given me his key so I knocked on the door, opened it, and walked into the room. Every light was on. The overhead ceiling light, bathroom light, desk light, and bedside light were burning brightly. I looked around and said, "Jeez, how can you sleep in here with every light on?" Then I remembered, "Hey, he's blind. It's all the same to him."

We got to the Toronto Airport in plenty of time but Customs decided that it was my day to get hassled. I was in full Sixties hippie mode with jeans, boots, and hair below my shoulders. Taking their time to process me, they searched my bag and made me take off my boots. By the time they were finished, I knew that we only had minutes to make it to our flight which was at a distant gate down the concourse.

I took the Reverend's guitar and both of our suitcases under my left arm, grabbed him by the elbow with my right hand, and started to run for the plane. In these times of political correctness, I shudder at the memory of racing down the corridor with Reverend Davis and shouting at the top of my voice, "Running with a blind man! Running with a blind man! Get out of my way, I'm running with a blind man!"

People flattened themselves against the walls as we rushed past them. We reached the gate gasping for air. I fell against the counter and handed over our tickets. Everyone stood watching us with their eyes wide and mouths agape. They held the plane for us anyway.

🔊 *Previous*
Reverend Gary Davis at the Club 47, Cambridge, 1963

Opposite 🔊
Reverend Gary Davis, Newport, (1) 1965 and (2) 1966

Cambridge, 1963

JESSIE

*J*esse Fuller was a folk blues artist who made his home in San Francisco. When the folk music craze hit big in the early 1960s, he was already on the scene and began to find more work at festivals. One of his songs, "San Francisco Bay Blues," was covered by Peter, Paul and Mary, and it crossed over from the niche folk genre into a major pop music hit.

Nicknamed "Lone Cat," Jesse wasn't the friendliest man in the world. He wasn't much for small talk and avoided the company of people who did not interest him (which was pretty much everybody). He built a small wooden hut on the back of his pickup truck to stay in when he was on the road.

Jesse had just returned home from some road dates when he got a call from manager Manny Greenhill informing him that Peter, Paul and Mary wanted him to join them in New York to sing "San Francisco Bay Blues" on live television. The network would pay for his airfare and hotel room. Jesse told Manny to give him the address in New York City and the time to be there.

He got into his truck and started driving east to New York. He met Peter, Paul and Mary and rehearsed the song that they later played live for a national audience. Jesse stayed around long enough to get his check, and then he got back into his pickup truck to drive back to San Francisco.

FULLER

Opposite
Jessie Fuller, Cambridge, 1963

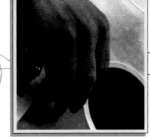

J O H N

This is the son of the great John Hammond. He is not John Hammond, Jr.—they have different middle names. People have always assumed that the younger John made a career of doing the material of blues artists who were rediscovered in the 1960s. In fact, he released his first album on Vanguard in 1962, before Son House, Skip James, Mississippi John Hurt and Booker White were found and brought back to performing. When John Hammond was doing their material, they were considered musicians who had made a few scratchy 78s and then vanished, leaving no legacy or musical shadow across the blues landscape. His album brought attention to this particular genre of music and contributed to the folk-blues boom of 1964–66.

After I discovered Son House in June, 1964, he was invited to the Newport Folk Festival. He fell ill, so his first appearance was scheduled for the Philadelphia Folk Festival in late August. When I asked John if he was going to be at Philadelphia, he mentioned that he was playing instead at the Gaslite that weekend. After Son finished his festival appearance on Sunday afternoon, I decided that we would pay John a visit on our way home to Rochester.

The Gaslite was a long, narrow club. Right past the side of the stage was a well-lit aisle leading to the dressing room. Son and I came into the club, waited until John had finished a song, and then slowly came down the aisle. Then John and I had what must have been one of the shortest conversations in history.

As Son and I moved into the light, John stared at Son, turned towards me, and asked, "Is it?"

I nodded my head seriously. "It is," I replied.

H A M M O N D

Opposite

JOHN HAMMOND, NEWPORT FOLK FESTIVAL, 1963

Cambridge, 1964

BOB DYLAN

ack in 1964, Joan was a bigger act than Bob and was headlining major concerts with him as the opening act. The situation was complicated due to their personal relationship, which ricocheted high and low by the day, sometimes by the hour. After performing in a show in Boston Commons, they came across the bridge to Cambridge. Joan had always been a favorite at the Club 47 where she first got her start in the late 1950s. Bob and Joan were having some romantic discord in the dressing room when someone popped in and asked Bob if he would come up and do a few songs.

Dylan and Mel Lyman, the harmonica player, went on stage and started to play. Dylan had done only a song or two when Joan walked down a side aisle and quietly slipped onstage behind him. She put her left hand on his back and then put her head down. Dylan knew exactly who it was behind him but he ignored her and kept playing.

Crouched by the side of the stage, I brought my camera up as Joan started to cry. I finished the roll of film and had it developed the next day. I was in a deep quandary as to whether to use the photos or not, so I locked the negatives away for almost 40 years. I finally decided that I should go ahead and show them, since I had not gone into their dressing room to invade their private space. They had brought their unhappiness out in public and put it on stage right in front of me.

Does this photograph deserve to be in this book of blues artists? When I looked at the misery and abject despondency in Joan's face as captured in the picture, I said to myself, "Hell, yes, it's got to be in there."

Opposite
Bob Dylan and Joan Baez, Cambridge, 1964

& JOAN BAEZ

Memphis, 1964

F U R R Y

During the summer of 1964, Nick Perls, Phil Spiro, and I went in search of Son House. On our way down to Mississippi, we spent a few days in Memphis and met Furry Lewis. In spite of his lengthy recording career, Furry had never really made any money and survived with a job as a sanitation worker, sweeping the streets of Memphis. With a wooden leg, he would sweep, limp, hop, and sweep again, continuing like that for hours.

Occasionally, advocates of Memphis music would put together a package tour for artists that would come to New York to play. I met Furry again at one of those concerts and found him in an especially bad mood. He said that a woman from California, Joni Mitchell, had recorded a song called "Furry Sings the Blues." He felt that she had appropriated his name and life without giving him anything in return.

I decided to do what I could for him, so I called Joni Mitchell's management office. I explained that Furry was upset by her profiting from his name and suggested that perhaps they might give him a share in the song. It obviously wasn't going to be any hit single, but it would bring in some money as the album sold. I proposed that they keep all of the publishing money but give Furry a half of the writer's credit. He would be getting a half of a half which might amount to a few hundred dollars twice a year. It wouldn't be much, but at least it would turn his thinking around and he would feel that he had a stake in the song. They responded that Ms. Mitchell had written both the words and music to the song and that, therefore, Mister Lewis was entitled to nada…zero. I always felt that for a few hundred bucks, he would have been proud to be mentioned in a song written by a woman who lived in faraway California.

Instead, Furry Lewis stayed bitter until the day he died.

L E W I S

Opposite
Furry Lewis, Memphis, 1964

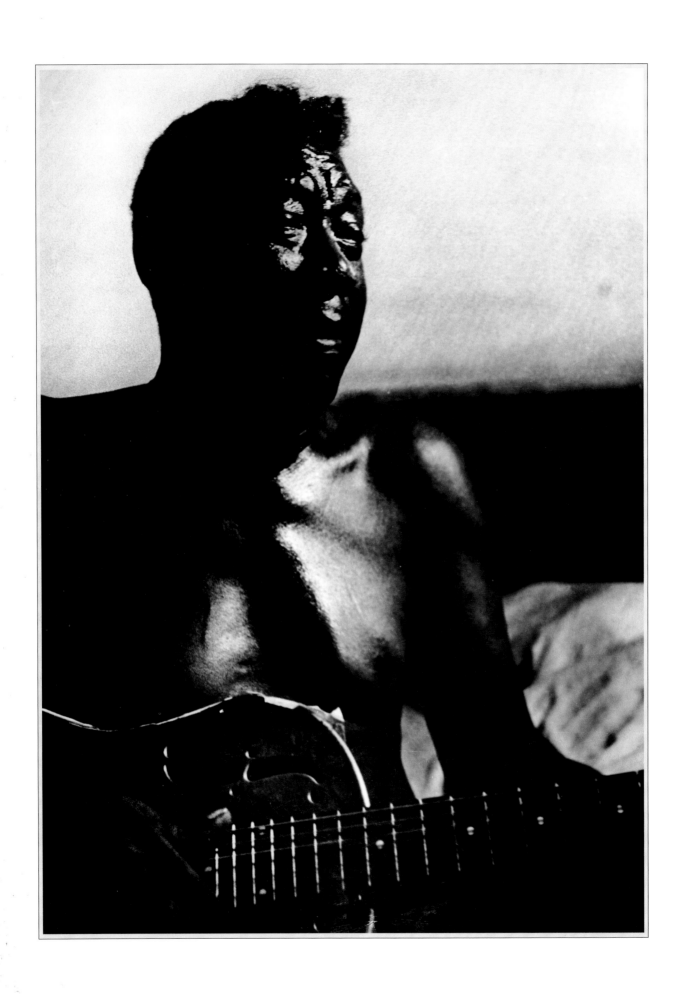

Memphis, 1964

While we were in Memphis that summer of 1964, Perls, Spiro, and I also visited Will Shade. Will had been the leader of the famed Memphis Jug Band and some of their songs ("He's in the Jailhouse Now" and "Stealin") were being performed by the Jim Kweskin Jug Band and other musicians on the 1960s folk music circuit.

Will lived in a squalid apartment at Beale Street and Fourth. It was torturous to haul our recording equipment up the stairs and get it set up to record him. He didn't have a guitar so we borrowed a steel-body National for him to use. Though he hadn't played much in recent years, his voice was strong and it was electrifying to hear those jug band songs being sung by the originator. While he was playing, I kept sneaking a look at his wife.

Jennie Shade was reputed to have been the most beautiful woman in Memphis. Men courted her avidly before she married Will. Now she was an aged woman rocking in her chair and sipping Calvert's Whiskey from a coffee cup. She chain smoked Pall Malls down to less than an inch and then lit a fresh one off of a butt.

Nick owned the tape recorder and gathered several hours of music while Phil and I sat and watched. Will was naked to the waist in the intense summer heat but he kept playing until Nick signaled that he was finished. As we were packing up the equipment, Phil and I exchanged glances and whispered that we should give Will some money. We had heard that music collectors from Scandinavia had come through Memphis in recent years and had paid as much as twenty dollars to record the local musicians. Since we were traveling on a budget, paying twenty dollars was totally out of our league, but we dug deep into our pockets and each came up with a five dollar bill which we gave him. Will didn't look at the money, but nodded his head in thanks and put it in his pocket.

As we headed back to the hotel in Nick's VW Beetle, Phil was in the passenger seat and I was squeezed into the back along with the recording gear. Nick turned to Phil and said, "You gave him money, didn't you?" Phil glanced back at me but didn't say anything. I leaned forward and replied, "Yeah, we gave him five bucks each. He gave us hours of his music so I figured that we should give him something for his work."

Nick shook his head slowly. "You just don't get it, do you?" he said. "He didn't give us shit. He's an old man with nothing happening in his life. We're the ones who gave him something."

Phil and I sat silently as Nick continued, "What the fuck was he going to do tonight? He was going to do nothing but sit and look at his old hag of a wife. We recorded his music and gave him the gift of immortality. Now his music will live on long after he's dead.

"He'll be dead soon but we have his music on tape. He gave us a couple of hours out of his empty life and we have given him eternity."

WILL SHADE

Opposite

WILL SHADE, MEMPHIS, 1964

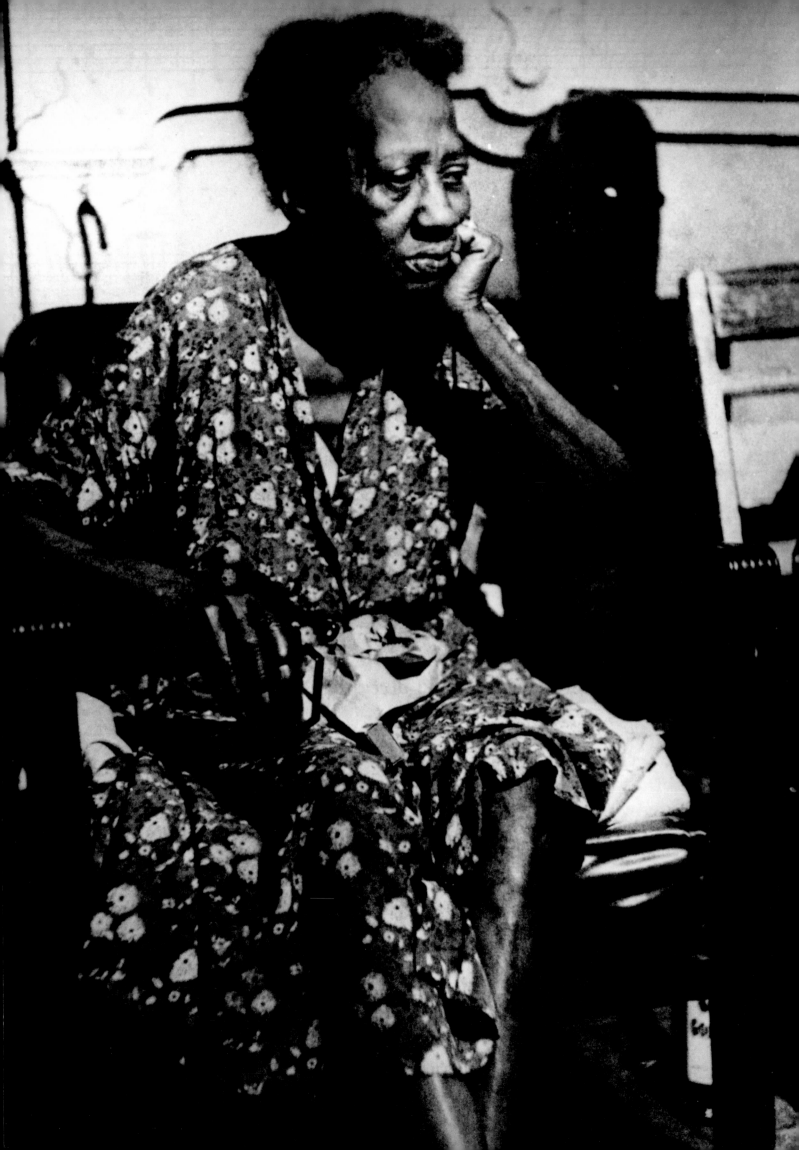

I closed my eyes and leaned back in the seat. What have I done? Did I believe that a human life was nothing more than a commodity to be squeezed for its final drop? I looked at the back of Nick's head as he drove through the night. I knew that we had at least two more weeks together before we would be home again.

That was a very long time to hate someone as much as I hated Nick Perls at that moment.

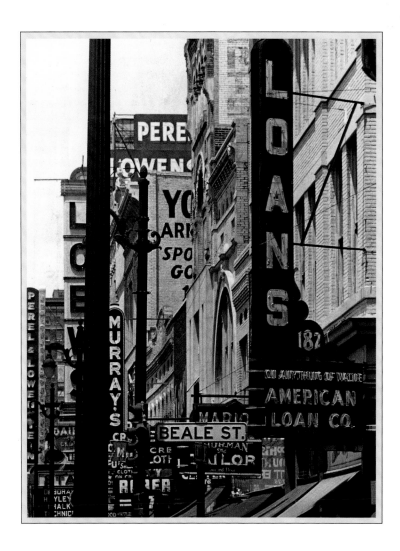

Opposite

JENNIE SHADE, MEMPHIS, 1964

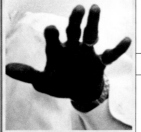

Newport Folk Festival, 1965

Lightning Hopkins was in his prime during the 1940s and 1950s. I worked with him in the 1960s when he had become a parody of himself. He had become more of an entertainer than a serious musician.

The older blues men gave Lightning a wide berth—they could never quite warm up to him. First of all, he was a city cat. He lived in Houston, while the others came from places called Rosedale, Avalon, Como, or Crawford. Secondly, Lightning played through an amplifier with a pickup on his guitar. Since everyone else was acoustic, Lightning could produce a more commanding sound with a lot less effort. Not to mention that he was an incredible flirt and would always play his songs directly to women in the audience.

I was backstage at the 1969 Ann Arbor Blues Festival when Evie House approached me. As the wife of Son House, her life was no picnic due to his heavy drinking. Mostly, she busied herself with going to church three or four times a week and reading the Bible at home. I had never seen her laugh out loud or show a crack in her dour demeanor.

Evie discreetly looked to one side and then the other before leaning towards me. "Dick, do you know that Lightning Hopkins man?"

I told her that I wouldn't say we were close friends, but I had known him for many years. She ground the toe of her shoe into the dust and then looked at me.

"Would you take me over and introduce me to him?"

Was I hearing things? Was the woman that Son referred to as "churchified" actually asking to meet Lightning Hopkins? I took her by the elbow and we walked over to where Lightning was holding court. With processed hair and sunglasses on at night, he was dressed in a shark-skin suit and held a cigar in one hand and a plastic cup of whiskey in the other.

"Lightning," I said, "I want you to meet my friend, Evie House."

He dropped the cigar and reached out his hand, taking Evie by the fingertips. He drew her to his side and looked up at her. "Hello, sweet thing," he whispered. "What's a young girl like you doing out here all alone?"

Evie put her hand to her face and started to giggle. She melted completely. Reading the Bible was the last thing on her mind. I took my leave at that point; I didn't want to be too close if a bolt of lightning came flashing down from the sky. Evie came up to me a few minutes later, sporting a wide grin with lights dancing in her eyes.

"That Lightning, he sure does say some pretty things to the ladies."

Lightning also liked his whiskey and we had a constant battle of wills about who was going to buy the bottle that he needed to play his gig. I didn't drink, but every time he had some con job going on me and I ended up paying. One evening, we were driving along on our way to a gig in Santa Monica when he pointed to a liquor store up the road.

"Hey, Dick, pull in here. I got to get me a little taste."

I pulled up in front of the store and turned to him with my palm up. "Money," I said.

"Aw, now Dick, I ain't got nothing but a hundred dollar bill."

I shook my head slowly. "They'll change it. Give me the hundred."

Lightning opened the door and got out of the car. He stood next to the open door and bent his head down to talk to me. "Dick, now you take a look at how Lightning is dressed tonight. Ain't I looking sharp?"

He was wearing a white suit, black shirt with a bolo tie, and black and white saddle shoes. I had to admit that he was looking fine. He stroked himself from his ribs down to his knee.

"Now looka here, ain't I looking good tonight? Now if you take my hundred dollar bill in there, what they goin' to give you back? I'll tell you what. They goin' to give you some big mess of dirty one dollar bills and five dollar bills.

"They gonna give you some ugly ass ball of dirty money for me to put back in my pocket."

He stroked his side again. "See how smooth ol' Lightning is lookin'? I can't be having it, Dick. I can't let them give me some big ball of dirty money because it would just mess up my line!"

I looked at him and shook my head in amazement. Lightning got me to buy the damn bottle again.

Previous

Lightning Hopkins, Newport Folk Festival, 1965

Opposite

Lightning Hopkins, Ann Arbor, 1969

Mance Lipscomb guitar detail

Mance Lipscomb was a sweet songster from Navasota, Texas, a small town about 90 miles from Houston. Navasota had one other celebrity musician and Mance was always happy to talk about him.

"You know who come from Navasota? Joe Tex lives there. You know he did that song, 'Who'll Take the Lady with the Skinny Legs'? Well, I seen him in town the other day and I called over to him. I said, 'Hey, Joe Tex, you know that lady with the skinny legs? Well, I'll take the lady with the skinny legs.' Man, he like to fall out laughing."

Mance had false teeth with the imprint of the state of Texas stamped on them. He was quick to whip them out and show them off proudly. He couldn't chew very well, so he was delighted whenever he stayed with me because my girlfriend at the time would make French Toast, one of the few things he could eat. Mance loved it so much that he asked for the recipe.

We explained it to him very carefully. "Break an egg, add a little milk, and whip it up. Put a piece of bread in it, turn it over, and soak both sides. Then put it in the pan and fry it up." He watched carefully and nodded his head. OK, he was sure that he knew how to make French Toast.

When he came back a few months later, we asked if he was enjoying French Toast at home. He shook his head sadly.

"My wife, she just couldn't make it right. You know how bad she made it?"

We looked at him and waited for the answer.

"She put it down on the floor and the dog wouldn't eat it!"

I *once had Mance booked to open for Big Mama Thornton at the University of Buffalo.* He was having a terrific night playing at his very best while Big Mama sat in the wings of the stage sipping out of a bottle of whiskey. The better he played, the madder she got. When he came off stage, she glared at him. There were 2,000 people screaming for an encore so Mance hurried back on stage and did another short song.

The second time he came off stage, the crowd rose to their feet, screaming for another song. Big Mama glared at him again and snarled, "You through, fool." Mance looked first at Big Mama, then at the 2,000 people hollering his name.

Turning back to Big Mama, Mance nodded his head. "You right, Big Mama. I is through."

Opposite

Newport Folk Festival, 1965

When I formed Avalon Productions in 1965, I did not realize that it was the first booking agency for blues artists. I knew that the blues had always been a token offering for agencies working with folk and jazz, but I never set out on any groundbreaking crusade. I would handle all personal appearances and notify the record companies of their artists' appearances so they could make sure to have stock in the stores. The labels loved this idea right from the beginning because booking dates for their artists was time-consuming and took their focus away from making records. I would charge more for the artists than they had been getting in the past. However, I would supply publicity photographs and press releases and make certain the travel itineraries were strictly observed.

Most of the artists had been victimized by the inhumane hiring practices of many clubs. The final straw for me was when I heard that Robert Pete Williams rode a bus from Baton Rouge to Los Angeles to work a weekend at the Ash Grove for $100, sat around in someone's apartment for five days, played a second weekend for another $100, and then took the bus back to Baton Rouge.

If Avalon Productions was going to work, I had to have absolute loyalty from the musicians themselves. They would have to reject direct bookings and tell club owners to call me. It was an incredible test of loyalty for men desperately in need of work, however meager. But every single one of them hung with me and refused to accept direct bookings.

Every one of them but Booker White.

Booker was staying with me in Cambridge when I put together his first lengthy tour of clubs. He started at The Pesky Sarpent in Springfield, Massachusetts, and then went on to New York, Philadelphia, and several other cities. The money was decent and I knew that I had done a good job. After all of the dates had been played, I was surprised that I didn't get any feedback from the clubs. Normally, I would have gotten some response one way or the other, but I didn't hear back from any of the places where he had played.

Some months later, I was talking to a friend from Springfield who casually mentioned noticing that Booker was coming back to The Pesky Sarpent. I called the club owner and asked what was happening. He said that Booker had complained about me right from the beginning. "Dick Waterman didn't play any music. Dick Waterman wasn't the one sweating on stage. Dick Waterman didn't do anything but stay at home and take ten percent of my money." Booker gave the owner his home phone number and said he would not come back unless business was done directly with him.

Coincidentally, at the same time, I had placed Booker on a Toronto television show being booked by Manny Greenhill. I got $500 for Booker to do a few songs on a show that would also feature Willie Dixon, Sunnyland Slim, Otis Spann, Brownie McGhee, and Sonny Terry. It was a real coup to have Booker on that show. I asked Manny if I could get extra money if they

B O O K E R
W H I T E

🔊 *Above*

BOOKER WHITE, NEWPORT FOLK FESTIVAL, 1965

went back into the tapes for a second show. He said that it was a "one shot." There would not be any reruns or a second show from unused tapes. "OK," I replied, "then it won't make any difference if there is a paragraph saying that Booker White gets paid another $500 if they decide to do a second show." Manny agreed to put the clause in the contract but it wouldn't matter because it wasn't going to happen.

Well, it happened. The show was so successful that they went back into the tapes to create another show. They also went back to check the paperwork. Spann, Dixon, and Sunnyland were free. McGhee,

Terry, and everyone else was free except for one $500 payment to Booker White. "Hey, no problem," they said and sent me a check for $500 before going forward with another show. I deposited the check into my account and mailed a check for $450 to Booker in Memphis.

Back in those liberal Sixties, there were many young white people who believed that every black musician was being robbed by every white manager. Booker had no problem in finding some well-meaning white person to send off an angry letter to CBC in Toronto demanding that Booker White receive the missing $50 that had been taken from him. CBC sent the letter on to me with a note stating that they had no involvement in the matter and I should take care of it directly.

I received the letter a week before the Newport Folk Festival where I had Booker playing. Furthermore, the matter of the $50 commission on the Canadian television show had come immediately on the heels of my discovery that he had told club owners to call him directly.

At Newport, I spotted Booker across an open field and walked directly towards the area where he was scheduled to play a workshop. When I got within about 50 feet, he turned to face me. The young white fans around him stepped back and opened a path for me to walk right up to him, face to face.

I took a fifty dollar bill and held it up for him to see. I folded it in half and stuck it in his shirt pocket. "Here is your money," I said. "Don't you ever speak my name again until they throw dirt over your dead body."

I made myself stare at him until he turned his head away. I never spoke to him again.

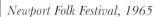
Newport Folk Festival, 1965

S L E E P Y

I didn't manage or book *Sleepy John Estes,* but I did try to help him out from time to time. It was difficult to find work for him because he was blind and always needed someone to pick him up in Brownsville, Tennessee, to bring him north.

Once, at a *Newport Folk Festival* in the 1960s, I was sitting and talking to him when someone brought him a check to pay him for playing. I asked him if he wanted me to cash it for him. John said that he would appreciate it, so I had the money broken down into small bills and returned to where he was sitting. I dropped down to one knee in front of him.

"Mister Estes," I said. "It's Dick Waterman, and I have your cash. Now give me your right hand."

He extended his right hand and I put a number of bills into it. "Now these are one dollar bills. Put them in your right pants pocket." He put the money away and extended his hand again. "These are five dollar bills.

Put these in your left pants pocket.

"Now here is the rest of your money, all in ten dollar bills. Take out your wallet and put these away in your wallet." John took his wallet from his back pocket, opened it wide, and put the bills into it.

"Ok, now tell me where your money is."

"I got one dollar bills in my right pants pocket. I got five dollar bills in my left pants pocket and the rest of the money is in ten dollar bills in my wallet."

"You got it just right. You be careful now and have a good trip home."

As I started to stand up, John reached out and took me by the forearm. "Mister Waterman," he said.

I dropped back down to one knee and looked into his dark glasses. "Yes, Mister Estes?"

"Thank you for doing that. No one ever fixed my money for me before."

J O H N   E S T E S

‹ *Opposite*

HAMMIE NIXON, YANK RACHELL, AND SLEEPY JOHN ESTES, NEWPORT FOLK FESTIVAL, 1965   *This is in the backstage area at the Newport Folk Festival, 1965. One of the sponsors was Ford Motor Company, which is why they're all wearing cheap plastic hats that say "Ford." That's Hammy Nixon on harmonica on the left, Yank Rachell playing mandolin in the middle, and Sleepy John Estes on the right.*

Carnegie Hall, New York, 1965

Chuck Berry *is a mercenary—you hire him and you get Chuck and his guitar.* You have to provide the band, an amplifier, the plane ticket, the hotel room, and whatever else is necessary. In those days, he came in as a hired gun. But with the sweat pouring off his face and that last drop hanging right on the tip of his chin, you could tell he worked very hard.

Chuck would always cut it pretty close, coming in almost at stage time. The promoter would meet him at the side of the stage, just behind the curtains so he could see the musicians. Right there, the promoter would count out the money in hundreds in front of him and Chuck would nod. Then he would undo his belt and drop his pants to knee level, stuff the hundreds in his money belt, pull up his pants, grab his guitar, and go on stage. There was your show.

The night I shot this photo, Chuck was performing at Carnegie Hall. He didn't have his own band, so he used Muddy Waters' band, which included Pewee Madison and James Cotton.

In the mid-1990s, I saw Mose Allison, whom I had also photographed that night, and said to him, "Gee, Mose, I got a picture of you in a show with Chuck Berry and Muddy Waters."

He replied, "Oh, yeah, yeah, yeah, back in the mid sixties. I did Carnegie Hall with them."

"Yeah, I saw the negative. I thought it was you," I said.

Mose continued, "I'll tell you something. I remember that show. Before Chuck came out, the band had already started playing on the two and the four, the two and the four, the two and the four.

"Chuck was introduced. He came out, put on his guitar, plugged in, and started playing on the one and the three, the one and the three, the one and the three. The band never came off the two and the four and Chuck never came off the one and the three."

The consummate musician, Mose Allison remembered that night when Chuck Berry and the Muddy Waters band played out of time with each other. Over thirty years later, it still bothered him.

CHUCK BERRY

Opposite

CHUCK BERRY AT CARNEGIE HALL, NEW YORK, 1965

MOSE ALLISON, NEW YORK, 1965

Cambridge, 1966

Brownie McGhee and Sonny Terry were the perfect example of two individuals in a wonderful partnership that just went on for too long. They started to play together in the 1930s and enjoyed about 30 years of both friendship and musical success. Towards the end of the 1960s, however, the relationship was starting to come apart and they had little contact with each other when they were not performing.

Brownie was a great guitarist who played in the tradition of his mentors, Blind Blake and Blind Boy Fuller. He was partially crippled and wore a shoe with a raised heel to even off his walk.

In my opinion, Sonny was the most underappreciated harmonica player of all time. Like Sonny Boy Williamson and Little Walter, Sonny Terry ranks as an originator whose influence extended far and wide. No one comes close to him in the East Coast style.

By their final years together, Brownie and Sonny were no longer considered a duo. Obviously incompatible, Brownie lived in Oakland, California, and Sonny lived in Long Island, New York. Their agency issued separate contracts and made it very clear that you were hiring two individual musicians contracted to perform simultaneously. They were not a duo.

After Sonny passed away, Brownie enjoyed some measure of success in the rock scene, working with Hot Tuna and other groups in the Bay Area. In 1995, Barry Dolins from the Chicago Blues Festival told me that he wanted to honor the great year of 1915 (which saw the births of Muddy Waters, Billie Holiday, Willie Dixon, Memphis Slim, Josh White and many others) but was unable to reach Brownie who had not performed in over seven years. Coincidentally, I had just helped Brownie get a nice payment for the use of about 20 seconds of his Jackie Robinson song in Ken Burns's baseball documentary series.

I called Brownie and said that he should play the Chicago festival because the money would be good and it was time for him to come out of . . . I started to use the word "retirement" but he exploded at me on the first syllable.

"Don't be using that word," he shouted. "I ain't retired."

"OK," I replied. "What shall we call the seven years that you haven't played?"

"They just ain't showed me the proper consideration."

"Ahh, yes," I thought to myself. "That money thing does raise its head." I knew that Barry was ready to offer $7,500 plus airfares and hotel rooms so I asked Brownie what he needed to make the date happen.

He paused and then replied, "I want $5,000." I told him to take

BROWNIE

McGHEE &

SONNY TERRY

Barry's call to work out the details. I could have been a middle agent on the deal and made a commission from both sides but I just stepped back and let them work it out themselves.

Brownie played the festival and was magnificent. He played alone, and then with Jerry Ricks, as well as Dave Meyers. He was jovial and outgoing on stage, talking about Big Bill Broonzy as he moved into "Key to the Highway." The performance was a triumph in every way and Brownie returned to Oakland in fine spirits. Barry had pulled off a major coup by having him there.

A few months later, I got a call from Brownie. He was choosing his words carefully. "That thing that you did for me in Chicago. Uhhh, you think you could get more of them?"

I answered that the 1995 season was finished but there was no question that he could make some very serious money if he wanted to take some outdoor festival dates the following year.

"Well, I don't have any agent and since I been knowing you for so long, I thought maybe you might want to look around and see what's out there."

I hadn't worked as an agent for some years and was living a quiet life in Mississippi. But when a $5,000 per show living legend asks you to be his agent, it suddenly becomes time to bring those ponies out of the barn and get the wagon fixed up and ready to roll again.

"I'll think about it," I said.

Brownie's health started to deteriorate around Christmas of that same year. He went downhill quickly and died in February. I flew out to Oakland for his funeral, the only one I ever attended in which the music of the deceased was played at the service. The burial site was miles away on the interstate coming out of San Francisco and moving past Berkeley. The procession got rolling right in the middle of rush hour, and we were immediately trapped in traffic that was five lanes across with everyone hurtling along at close to 70 miles an hour. White knuckled in the front seat and pointing straight ahead, I yelled, "Follow that hearse! Follow that hearse!".

SONNY TERRY AND BROWNIE MCGHEE, CAMBRIDGE, 1966 *One of my favorite "in" jokes takes place in the film The Color Purple. There is a scene in a juke joint where three men are sitting at the bar when a really foxy young thing walks behind them, wearing a tiny dress and looking mighty fine. The three men turn in unison and watch her move past them. The man in the middle murmurs, "My, my, she is lookin' fine to me." That man is Sonny Terry, totally blind and playing the scene for all it's worth.*

Fred McDowell guitar detail

Fred McDowell was the Will Rogers of the blues world. There were no such things as "strangers" to Fred. They were just friends that he hadn't met yet. He spoke in a rapid drawl, starting each sentence with "Well, now, looka here." We remained friends ever since our first meeting at the 1964 Newport Folk Festival. I would call him for occasional festival bookings whenever I had anything for him.

By the late 1960s, he was doing quite well on European tours and taking independent recording contracts for cash. He had just come back from an especially successful tour of England when I heard that he was working at Stuckey's (a southern chain of gas stations and restaurants) for $32 a week. Bewildered as to why he would need a job that paid so little, I called and asked him why he was doing it.

"Well, now, looka here, Dick. I get up in the morning and all my friends is hanging out at Stuckey's, so I just go out there and set with them all day. Now if it get to runnin' busy, they'll give me a holler and say, 'Hey, Fred, go fill up that Cadillac at pump five.'

"So they are payin' me thirty-two dollars a week to do what I would be doin' anyway.

"Looka here, Dick, I am flat out *stealin'* their money!"

At the 1969 Ann Arbor Blues Festival, Bonnie Raitt, Fred, and I had rooms on the same floor of a hotel. Bonnie and I were coming back from dinner when she said that she wanted to knock on

Fred's door to say "Goodnight" to him. I assured her that he was just fine but she was concerned that he was sitting in his room feeling lonely because he was a long way from home. Despite my assurances, Bonnie insisted on knocking on the door.

No answer.

She knocked again, harder. Still no answer.

With deep concern in her eyes, Bonnie pounded on the door with her fist.

The door flew open and the smell of marijuana, cigarettes, and stale beer came rushing out to envelop us. About 40 people were in Fred's hotel room, in full revelry on the beds, beside the beds, between the beds, and under the beds. Fred, surrounded by a bevy of nubile college girls, was sitting on a bed playing guitar. He looked at the door and waved at us.

"Hey, looka here, everybody. That's Bonnie and Dick. Come on in!"

Bonnie shook her head, stepped back and closed the door.

As we walked down the hall, I slowed down and let her move ahead of me. I started to talk to her softly, "Poor Fred…got no friends…staying in his room alone…lonesome Fred…sad and lonely Fred."

She stayed pissed at me for days.

Fred had been feeling poorly for some time when I finally convinced him to see a doctor in early 1972. The next day, he called me back to say that he had been diagnosed with cancer. He was going to start che-

FRED McDOWELL

motherapy treatments in Memphis, but the outlook was not good.

Meanwhile, I was in a royalty fight with my good friend Manny Greenhill over the Rolling Stones' recording of "You Got to Move." The Stones stated that they were doing Fred's version of the song. Manny, however, was holding fast that his client, Reverend Gary Davis, had a copyright on a song of the same title.

With Fred dying of cancer, it was urgent that I get a sizable sum of money to him as soon as possible. We hammered out a deal according to which Fred got 75% of the royalties and Reverend Davis got the other 25% for no reason at all. If anyone ever did the Reverend's version of the song, Fred would get 25% of the royalties. But fate plays cruel tricks. While Fred was battling cancer in a Memphis hospital, Reverend Davis had a massive stroke and died first in May, 1972.

About two months later, I received a phone call from a doctor in Memphis. "I just wanted you to know that your friend, Mister McDowell, fought very bravely but he died of cancer this morning."

As I put down the phone, I wondered, "What kind of man is so magically connected that his doctor makes long distance calls to inform the man's friends that he has died?"

Bonnie was in Woodstock at the time making her second album. I called the studio and spoke to Michael Cuscuna, who was producing the record. I told him that it was important to inform her of Fred's death. Michael replied that all of the recording had been done and they were in the crucial mixing stage. Any distraction would delay the album. I let him know that he was running the risk of someone walking into the studio and casually mentioning that Fred McDowell had died. Michael had to take Bonnie aside and break the news to her.

Later, I heard that she went into the cabin where she was living and stayed inside all day and all the following night. She emerged the next morning and told Michael that she was ready to resume work. That album, *Give It Up*, is regarded by many as her best work.

It is dedicated to Fred McDowell.

FRED MCDOWELL GRAVESTONE

Previous

MISSISSIPPI FRED MCDOWELL, ANN ARBOR, 1969

Above

SAM HINTON, DOC WATSON, REV. DAN SMITH, MISSISSIPPI FRED MCDOWELL, AND TAJ MAHAL, NEWPORT FOLK FESTIVAL, 1967

Cambidge, 1964

Over 40 years have passed, but I can remember his menacing presence as if it was yesterday. I can still clearly see a huge muscular black man standing chest to chest with me (actually his chest to my chin) and his voice rolling up from the depths of his fury.

"What…you…been…doing…for…*the folks*?!"

Taj Mahal was after my ass again.

When I first met Taj back in the 1960s, he was Henry Fredrickson, a student at the University of Massachusetts who played banjo and barrelhouse piano at folk clubs in Cambridge. Later, when I was managing the older blues musicians, Taj was their self-appointed protector, guardian, gatekeeper, and high sheriff. He made it his business to get next to them and make certain that they were being treated honestly and fairly.

Which always put him in my face.

It was the same snarling confrontational question.

"What…you…been…doing…for…*the folks*?!"

I always shook my head and gave him the same answer. "Look, Taj, I'm not frightened or intimidated, (yeah, right!). I'm just going to keep on doing what I'm doing."

"You can threaten me all you want. Just leave me alone and let me get my work done."

Taj would poke my chest with his finger and have the final word. "If I ever find that you're fuckin' with *the folks*, I'll come after you and beat your ass bloody."

So much for human kindness.

As the years went by, the blues men continued to speak well of me and how I conducted my business on their behalf. I saw Taj less often as the blues men either retired or passed away during the 1980s and 1990s. In recent years, he has become involved with the Music Maker Foundation and uses his popularity to headline tours for Etta Baker, Cootie Stark, Beverly Watkins, and other musicians based in the Carolinas.

Taj has performed in countless incarnations, ranging from solo acts to Caribbean combos and full bands with horn sections. Restlessly creative, he is always seeking new musical genres to explore and bring to audiences. Although mellowed from his days as Lord High Protector of the blues, he remains firmly placed on an ethical level high above the mainstream. There will be no disrespectful behavior toward any traditional musician while Taj Mahal is on his watch.

I was at the 2003 Poconos Blues Festival when I was grabbed from behind while walking up a flight of stairs. Huge arms were wrapped around me and a head loomed over my shoulder. That voice—that very same voice—came across four decades and rumbled into my ear.

"What…you…been…doing…"

I spun around and hugged him as we yelled the final words aloud to each other.

"For . . *the folks*!"

We laughed, joked, and talked about old times. Where there had been suspicion, there was now trust. Where there had been confrontation, there was now a valued friendship.

But that does not erase the sound that has stayed with me for over four decades.

"What…you…been…doing…"

Taj was one scary son of a bitch back then.

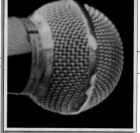

Big Joe Williams was the sav- viest, most street smart person I ever worked with. He could neither read nor write, yet he drove himself all over the country and apparently never lost his way. How did he know which turnpike exit to take or which street to turn onto? How did he manage to find a coffeehouse in Steamboat Springs or a club in downtown Philadelphia?

Back in the 1930s, when recording artists were taking just a few dollars for the copyright and publishing of their songs, Joe had an innate sense of what was his and the need to hold onto it. Joe's wallet was several inches thick but he knew what every piece of paper in it meant. Once, he took out a folded letter and said that it was from a record company in England who wanted to record one of his songs. I read the paper and it was a request from Parrot Records for Tom Jones to record "Baby, Please Don't Go." Decades after Joe wrote that song, I helped him fill out the renewal form to extend his copyright. The song had been split up so many times that he was only getting an eighth or a twelfth of the original ownership, but he still collected his checks twice a year.

At one point, two of the Chambers Brothers and Joe were staying in my apartment in Cambridge. We got to talking about fried chicken when Joe announced that he would do the cooking if I bought the chicken and left him alone in the kitchen. I brought back a huge mound of cut up chicken pieces and he already had pots of cooking oil in full boil on the stove. He cut open a paper bag and filled it with white flour and lots of black pepper.

We offered to help but he banished us from the kitchen. Big Joe stood over the stove with his shirt off, wearing a sleeveless undershirt. He would rinse the chicken, throw it into the flour, and toss it several times until it was well coated. Next he would drop each piece into the boiling oil, sending cascades of foaming heat upward. Each time he finished six or eight pieces of chicken, he would bring them out into the living room and then return to his labors.

It was a meal to die for.

It wasn't just great fried chicken. It was perhaps the best fried chicken that I have ever had in my life.

The following morning I was standing at the stove making coffee and remembering that wonderful chicken when something dropped into my hair. I looked up at the ceiling and it was dimpled with hundreds of drops of cold cooking oil that had congealed there after wafting upwards from Joe's cooking. I got a sponge mop and cleaned off the ceiling, still feeling that I had gotten the much better end of the deal.

BIG JOE

WILLIAMS

Above

BIG JOE WILLIAMS, ANN ARBOR, 1969

B O B B Y

There is no question that airplay for blues artists is segregated and not likely to get any better within the foreseeable future. There is no chance that Buddy Guy, Robert Cray, or Shemekia Copeland is going to get played on the black radio stations across the southern part of the United States. These artists appeal to upscale white audiences who buy their CDs and see them in northern clubs and festivals.

The airwaves of black stations are filled with the music of a number of black recording artists who are eager to break away from playing southern roadhouses and jukes, and gain a foothold in the white festival market of the north. But mostly they live off of the southern circuit, playing black clubs and lounges from Georgia across to Texas. That's the real cake.

The frosting is if you play at a festival that has a large white audience, like the Poconos Festival or the Waterfront Festival in Portland, where the money and audiences are good.

Some artists have been able to maintain their credibility with black radio stations while gradually increasing their opportunities to play outside of the south. Among these are Little Milton, Bobby Rush and, of course, Bobby Bland. Bobby Bland is one of the great love ballad singers of all times and when he comes to the front of the stage and makes eye contact with women in front of him, it is unlike anything since Frank Sinatra back in the 1940s. He is a very classy man and he carries himself with a sense of dignity as he moves along his musical path, trying to play a few less road houses and few more wealthy festivals.

B L A N D

Opposite

BOBBY BLAND, ANN ARBOR, 1969

Signing documents, 1971

Around 1968 Bob Koester of *Delmark Records* told me that he was recording Arthur "Big Boy" Crudup and asked if I would take on the job of finding him some festival work. I went to Chicago to meet Arthur and found him to be a genuinely nice man. Quiet and polite, it was clear he felt that he had lived a hard life without much chance of it getting better. Over the next few years, I found Arthur some bookings, but he was a lackluster performer. In spite of the great material, he was wooden on stage and had little audience rapport.

I was aware that he had written several songs recorded by Elvis Presley, including Elvis's first hit, "That's All Right, Mama." Most of Arthur's early material had been recorded by Lester Melrose on Blue Bird. Lester held the publishing rights through Wabash Music Co. I asked Arthur if he had been getting royalty checks. He surprised me by replying that he had been receiving checks infrequently for very small amounts—twelve, nine, or eighteen dollars. I enrolled him in an organization called the American Guild of Authors and Composers (AGAC), whose New York City office was headed up by a man named John Carter. Carter worked hard to help Arthur get back royalties.

Lester Melrose had turned Wabash Music over to a company named Hill & Range before retiring to Florida. He died there a few years later, leaving his wife as heir to his estate.

Around 1972, Carter notified us that he had reached a settlement with Hill & Range. I came down to New York from Cambridge. Arthur got up before dawn and, accompanied by his daughter and three sons, drove up from Virginia. The children would have to sign the papers as well to ensure Hill & Range that Arthur's heirs were in agreement with the settlement.

We gathered in the office of the Hill & Range lawyer to sign the papers. The lawyer took them upstairs to be signed by the company president and planned to return with a check for $60,000. While we were shaking hands and hugging each other, Arthur sat quietly and just watched the door. Ten minutes went by and then twenty. We became anxious after a half-hour passed. The door opened and the Hill & Range lawyer walked in, his face pale and showing obvious signs of distress. He walked behind his desk and looked down for a few seconds before saying to Arthur, "He won't sign the agreement. He says that it gives away more in settlement than you could hope to get through litigation."

Carter came out of his seat and argued heatedly but it was to no avail. We were not going to get any $60,000. We were not going to get anything at all. Arthur turned to me, knowing that I would explain it to him in a way that he could understand.

"Look, Arthur, they are refusing to give you money in a settlement and they are saying that you can sue them if you want. But that means going after an old white widow who lives in Florida. We wouldn't have a chance of winning a case against her."

ARTHUR CRUDUP

We took the elevator downstairs. Arthur and I stood on the sidewalk together as his children huddled against the building in the October cold. The wind was blowing hard off of the river and they were not dressed for the severe weather. I stood in front of Arthur and told him several times how sorry I was. I told him over and over that we would get them and make them pay for what they had done to him.

Arthur reached out and took my hands and folded them inside of his own huge hands. He looked me in the face and spoke slowly. "I know you done the best that you could. I respects you and I honors you in my heart. But it just ain't meant to be."

He motioned his head upwards at the buildings above us. "Them people got their ways of keeping folks like me from getting any money. If they was to bring me green money and say 'Take this and fold it up in your hand,' well, then I guess I'd know that I had me something.

"Naked I come into this world and naked I shall leave it. It just ain't meant to be. I know you done your best and I honor you in my heart for everything."

He stepped back and looked at his children shivering in the cold. "I 'spect we better start driving now. We got us a ways to go."

Arthur died the following spring and I drove down to Virginia for his funeral. Many of the mourners took the time to tell me that Arthur had spoken very highly of me. On the way back to Cambridge, I stopped in New York City and went to the office of the lawyer that I had used to negotiate Bonnie Raitt's contract with Warner Brothers. While I was waiting, I started to talk to one of his associates and brought forth all of the disgust and loathing that I felt for what had happened to Arthur.

The associate listened carefully, took notes, and then announced a plan. "The first thing that we'll do is shut off the money spigots to keep the record companies from paying any further royalties to Hill & Range."

We did that and waited for Hill & Range to come to the bargaining table. Then we got a stroke of luck. Chappell Music was in the process of buying Hill & Range when they discovered that there was an outstanding legal dispute with the Crudup estate. Chappell refused to go forward with the deal until the matter was settled. We finally had the leverage that we needed.

The settlement agreement was negotiated quickly. The estate would get back royalties and ownership of the songs when they came up for copyright renewal. I was in the office when the first check was issued. It was for slightly over $248,000, more than four times what Hill & Range had refused to pay. Over the past 30 years, the estate has been paid around three million dollars. People ask me if I am happy about how it turned out. I tell them that, honestly, I don't give it much thought.

I just think back to that cold afternoon when a very gentle man held my hands in his and said he honored me in his heart because I had done the best that I could for him.

⌐ *Previous*
ARTHUR CRUDUP, MELBOURNE, AUSTRALIA, 1971

Opposite ⌐
ARTHUR CRUDUP SIGNING DOCUMENTS, NEW YORK, 1972

Following ⌐
BONNIE RAITT AND ARTHUR CRUDUP

Ann Arbor, 1969

In the late 1960s, I was already managing Buddy Guy and Junior Wells when Luther Allison approached me and asked if he could join my roster. He was a brilliant guitarist and fine vocalist, as well as especially hard-working in his public appearances. He was the first blues artist signed to Motown Records. Even Mick Jagger had expressed admiration for Luther as an artist.

The only problem was that Luther wanted everyone to like him. He was continually talking to managers, agents, promoters, lawyers, and anyone else whom he felt could help him move up in the music business. He wasn't intentionally disloyal; he just couldn't help self-promoting.

I had my doubts as to whether he would be a good fit with Buddy and Junior, two hard working musicians who had proven their loyalty to me many times over the years. Nonetheless, I convinced myself that Luther was just being an overly enthusiastic puppy who meant no harm. As I am genuinely fond of other people who love and care for him deeply, I won't get into the details of Luther's disloyalty to me. Suffice it to say that he dealt me a staggering financial blow that wiped out of all of my savings and left me hanging on by my fingernails for several years.

Shortly after our falling out, Luther moved to Europe and I didn't see him or hear anything about him for over 20 years. Around 1994, I was backstage at a B.B. King and Bobby Bland concert at the University of Mississippi when Leo "Tater Red" Allred walked up to me. He said that Luther Allison was there and wanted to talk to me. Luther was making an album in Memphis and had come down for the show.

I looked at Leo and shrugged. "I'm just a guy watching a show. I don't care who talks to me."

A few minutes later, Luther walked up and stood next to me. Neither one of us offered his hand in friendship as we stood silently watching the concert.

Finally, he stepped in front of me and turned to face me. "Look, man, I messed up and I know that I put you in a bad way. I don't expect you and me will ever be friends again, but I just want you to know that it's been on my mind all these years. I was listening to the wrong people but that don't excuse what I done."

I waited a few seconds, turned toward him, and extended my hand. "You're right in saying that we'll never be friends again. But I hope your new album does well and I wish you a lot of success now that you're back in the country."

Luther's career soared over the next few years and he was able to reach headliner status at the major blues festivals. However, his comeback was brief because he was diagnosed with brain cancer in the spring of 1997 and passed away just weeks later. When he died, I wondered why I did not feel any great sadness. The blues community is small and the loss of any talented musician should be a time for mourning.

Then I realized that I was a doubly flawed man. I could never forgive disloyalty and I would carry a grudge to the very end.

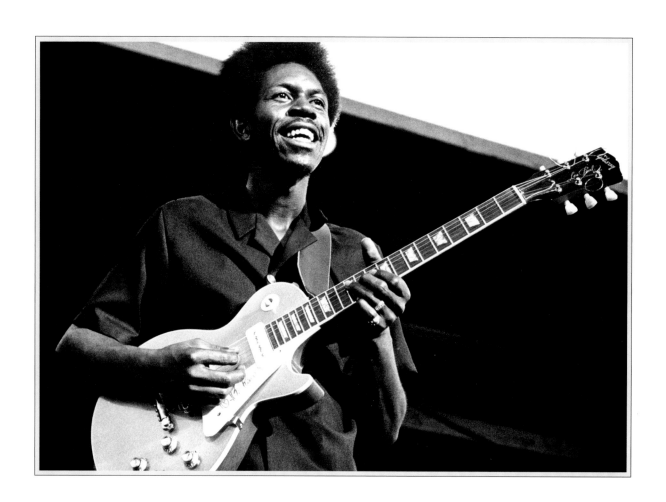

Above 🔊

LUTHER ALLISON, ANN ARBOR, 1970

🔊 *Previous*

LUTHER ALLISON, ANN ARBOR, 1969

Opposite 🔊

LUTHER ALLISON AND JOHN LEE HOOKER, SAN FRANCISCO, CA, 1995

Ann Arbor, 1969

Albert could be abrasive and unpredictable. There were times when he almost welcomed photographers to the front of the stage. But when he was in a bad mood, he would threaten to shut down his show unless all cameras were gone from the audience. He could be hell on soundmen; in many instances he was justified, but often he used technical difficulties just to gain audience sympathy.

In the 1960s, Albert played The Scene, a New York City club owned by Steve Paul where you could be certain that Jimi Hendrix would show up if he was in town. Hendrix loved to get on stage and play bass behind Albert, laying down a much more melodic line than the standard bass player. I knew Jimi pretty well and whenever I saw him he would quiz me about Albert King and Otis Rush. He was especially curious about Otis, a brilliant singer and searing guitarist who lacked the business acumen to sustain any sort of a road career. After one particularly long question-and-answer session with Jimi about Albert and Otis, I finally reached my exasperation point.

"Look, Jimi," I said, "What is it with you asking about Albert and Otis all the time? What is it about them that is so intriguing to you?"

"Hey, man," he looked at me and smiled, "it's a left-handed thang."

A couple of decades later, I was promoting a John Lee Hooker show at the New Daisy Theater in Memphis. I was paying too much for John Lee but reasoned that he had not appeared in Memphis in many years. Advance sales were mediocre, but I could break even or perhaps make a few bucks if I had decent walk-up sales on the night of the show.

As I got out of my car to go into the club for the sound check, someone waved at me from across the street. "Hey, Dick, did you hear? Albert King has announced that he's retiring and tonight is his final performance." I was stunned but I didn't believe it for an instant. I walked up to the box-office window and stuck my head through the hole.

"How we doing?"

"We suck. Everybody's going over to West Memphis for Albert King's final performance."

"Now wait just one goddam minute here," I thought. "Albert King has a wife, a mistress, and a bunch of girl friends. He plays blues guitar and shoots crap for big money in the back room of every bar in town. So what the hell is he going to do with his life if he retires?"

I'll tell you what the hell he is going to do. Albert King is going to keep a wife, a mistress, and a bunch of girlfriends. He is going to play blues guitar and shoot crap for big money in the back room of every bar in town. Albert King is never going to retire, he is just going to kill my John Lee Hooker date and then keep on screwing, strumming, and shooting crap for the rest of his life.

And that's exactly what he did.

Opposite
ALBERT KING, ANN ARBOR, 1969

Ann Arbor, 1969

Otis Rush is one of the most talented musicians ever to come out of Chicago. He is also one of the most inconsistent and unpredictable. He can lift his music to the heights in front of 15 people in Ames, Iowa, and then drop down to mediocre doodling in front of 20,000 at a festival.

After I had begun managing Buddy Guy and Junior Wells, I tried to book some gigs for Otis. The problem was that he never seemed to have his business together. Each time, he had a new and original excuse.

"The bass player called and canceled out on me."

"The guy with the trailer for the gear didn't show up."

"Is it tonight? I thought you said Saturday."

One memorable night, when I had booked him to play at the University of Rochester, my phone rang at about 8 P.M.

It was Otis looking for directions. "I can't find that school nowhere."

"Where are you?" I asked.

He turned away from the phone and I heard him ask a question. He came back on the line. "I'm in Westchester."

"Westchester!" I yelled. "You're supposed to be in Rochester!"

Otis was very calm and not at all upset. "Well, where should I go now?"

My mind was reeling. I had to save this big money gig. "Find the New York State Thruway and start driving north. Stay on it until you get to Rochester. You have a long way to drive, so get going!"

Then I called the school and got the entertainment chairman on the line. "Look, Otis has gone a little bit out of his way, so delay putting the opening act on stage for a while and let them play a long set. Let them play a very long set."

I still regard that as one of my finest moments as a booking agent. Otis arrived at the school at 1 A.M., played a set for a few dozen people, and collected his full payment.

Opposite

OTIS RUSH, CAMBRIDGE, 1971

Philadelphia, 1969

In 1956, Robert Pete Williams was sentenced to life in Louisiana's Angola Prison for killing a man. After serving two years, Dr. Harry Oster, a professor and ethnomusicologist at Louisiana State University, took a 12-string guitar to the prison and recorded Robert playing with Guitar Welch and Hogman Maxey. Singing about prison life, the music was haunting in its realism,

> *Some got six months,*
> *Some got a solid year,*
> *But me and my buddy*
> *We got a lifetime here.*

Robert's prison recordings earned him a pardon in 1959. His first appearance outside of the state of Louisiana was at the 1964 Newport Folk Festival, where I first met him. I approached him with some hesitation. He was sitting by the side of the stage, wearing a black wool suit with a dress shirt, tie, and a pork pie hat in the stifling July heat. Lines of sweat rolled down his face. I stood next to him and waited until he looked up at me.

"I have your Angola recordings, Mister Williams," I said. "It's nice to see you here. What happened to Mister Welch and Mister Maxey?"

He stared at me for a moment and then spoke, "They still there."

could hear his music in the distance, being played very softly. I couldn't figure out where he was. The entire apartment consisted of only one bedroom, a living room, a tiny kitchen, and a bathroom.

I finally realized that he was at the bottom of the stairs, playing his guitar and singing in a low voice that was barely a whisper. I took my camera and snapped a few pictures. When he heard the shutter go off, he immediately stopped playing and came up the stairs.

"That was really beautiful," I said, "That was soft and gentle, and it didn't sound like anything that you usually play."

Shaking his head, he replied, "Well, I warn't playin' no kind of real music. I was just puttin' my words in the air for Hattie Mae."

I nodded at the mention of his wife's name. "I thought it was lovely. What were you saying to her?"

He shrugged his shoulders. "I was just tellin' her that I had one more play with Mister Richard. I tell her that I love her and I tell her to make sure that the kids do their schoolwork. I tell her that I was gettin' on the bus tomorrow and that I was comin' home to her."

"You should play something

ROBERT
PETE WILLIAMS

In the late 1960s, I had a small apartment in Philadelphia and Robert was staying with me while he played the final date of a short tour. One morning, I woke up and

like that tonight. I think the people would really like to hear a song like that."

He shook his head again. "No, them people pay their money and they want to hear reels and buck dances and blues songs. I warn't playin' no kind of music. I was just puttin' my thoughts in the air for Hattie Mae to hear me."

Previous

ROBERT PETE WILLIAMS, PHILADELPHIA, 1969

Above

MISSISSIPPI FRED MCDOWELL, ARTHUR CRUDUP, AND ROBERT PETE WILLIAMS, BUCKS COUNTY, PA, 1970

Once, while he was staying with me, he insisted on buying dinner one night. Unable to read or write, Robert shopped by the pictures on the labels of the boxes and cans. He brought home a large package of frozen macaroni and cheese. I cooked it up and put it on our plates. He poked it with his fork before looking at me.

"I don't see no meat in this. Whar the meat in this?"

"It's macaroni and cheese, Robert. There isn't any meat in it."

He got up from the table, took the box out of the trash, and brought the box back to the table. He studied it intently. Then he turned the box toward me. "Well, now, looka here. This here picture show meat in a sauce. Ain't that meat in a sauce?"

I looked at the picture and could see where the ridges of macaroni looked like slivers of cooked beef in a cream sauce.

"Look, Robert," I said earnestly, "It's macaroni and cheese and I really like it a lot, so you did buy the right thing for dinner. I'm enjoying this. Thanks for getting it."

Robert ate slowly and kept glancing at the empty box beside his plate.

Robert was dying of cancer in Earl K. Long Hospital in 1980 when I came to Baton Rouge with Bonnie Raitt for a concert. I took a cab to the hospital and walked into the reception area. I went up to the desk and told the woman that I was there to see Robert Williams.

She opened a small metal box and slowly worked her way through file cards until she reached the end. She shook her head. "We got a bunch of Robert Williams in here."

"He's dying of cancer," I added.

The woman reached for a different metal box and read them each slowly until she reached the last one. She stared at it for a moment and then looked up at me. "He's on Three West."

I took the elevator to the third floor and walked to the nurse's station. No one was there so I stood and waited for five minutes. After ten minutes had passed, I walked around the circular hallway and read the cards on the doors with the patient's names. I saw one that said, "Williams, R.P.," and entered the room. I walked between several metal trays and stood in front of him.

I hardly recognized him. He was wearing a white hospital gown that was open in the back. His huge muscular frame was shrunken and his arms and legs were thin and bony. I watched him breathe for a few minutes. As I turned to leave, I brushed against a metal tray stand and it scraped against the floor loudly. I froze and slowly turned back to look at Robert. He opened his eyes slowly, blinking several times to focus on me.

"Mister Richard," he whispered. "Is that you, Mister Richard?"

I stepped forward and touched the hospital bed. "I'm in town with Bonnie," I said softly. "She told me to tell you she sends her love."

He slowly replied, "You give Miss Bonnie a hello back. Tell her it come from Robert." His face was skeletal, making his eyes and teeth look huge. "Mister Richard, this cancer done et me up bad. Oh, man, it hurt me so much."

We talked softly for a while until he closed his eyes and fell silent. I waited a moment before slowly moving toward the door. I turned back around for one final look and his eyes were open.

"Mister Richard," he said, "If the good Lord lets me into His heaven, I will surely save you a place. When it come your time to be in heaven, you come be next to Robert."

I waited until he closed his eyes again. I took the elevator downstairs and got a cab back to the concert hall. The next time I came to Louisiana would be for his funeral.

O K, after all these years, I'll admit it.

I'm the one who told Buddy Guy to play Eric Clapton.

Buddy has been criticized for dabbling in the music of Clapton, Stevie Ray Vaughan, and Jimi Hendrix, among others. He samples their styles for audiences just to prove that he can play them. Some people enjoy this musical side trip, but many others feel that it is beneath Buddy's talent to showcase others when his own contributions are more than enough to satisfy any true blues fans.

Blame me. When I first brought Buddy out of Chicago around 1966, Cream was already a major rock act. Cream's lead guitarist, Eric Clapton, eagerly acknowledged that Buddy was his personal idol and a major influence on his guitar technique. I had to find a way to use this as currency to boost Buddy's career, so I sat down with Buddy and devised a plan. Let's show the world that you can play Clapton and then *not* do it.

The idea was this: Buddy would be ripping through some incredible guitar solo as he worked his way to the front of the stage. He would chop his guitar neck down and the band would instantly stop playing. Buddy would stand motionless on the lip of the stage and milk the silence.

Three seconds…five seconds…ten seconds…

And then he would slowly drip the opening notes to Cream's "Sunshine of Your Love." It would be Buddy's way of saying, "He says he can play me but I'm showing you that I can play him too." Then, just as the audience would begin to understand what Buddy was doing, he would turn toward the band, raise the guitar neck, and roar back into his blues song. The idea was not to play Clapton but just to show the crowd that he could if he wanted to. Good concept, bad execution. Buddy simply fell in love with the adulation that he got from playing the opening to "Sunshine of Your Love," and what had been intended as a tease became a focal point of his show.

For those who feel that his performances are full of flash and glitter, I can only tell them that the Buddy Guy of the mid-1960s was the most creative and innovative guitarist that I have ever seen. He would play a tiny Chicago Southside club called Theresa's and put on a display of visual dynamics that was beyond brilliant. He would stick the guitar into the asbestos pipes over the stage and play left-handed, then take out a handkerchief and whip the guitar that was hanging upside down. I saw him roar through a guitar solo and break a string, forcing him to adapt to five strings. When he broke another string, Buddy completely improvised on the remaining four. To this day, his level of technical expertise is underappreciated because he makes it all look so simple.

BUDDY GUY

Opposite
BUDDY GUY, CAMBRIDGE, 1968

Above

Buddy Guy and Robert Pete Williams, Philadelphia, mid-1970s

Opposite

Buddy Guy, New Orleans, 1995

London, 1969

In late 1964, Cream came to Boston *and played in a space* that used to be an underground parking garage. If ever there was an "acoustic hell on earth," this was the place. It was made of concrete and the reverberations were beyond description. It has been almost 40 years, but I am certain that anyone driving out on Kenmore Square on Massachusetts Avenue will still hear the faint echoes of "White Room."

I'm not sure when I first met Eric Clapton, but I already knew him by the time he played Boston. After the show, Eric and I went back to his hotel room. I had brought along an old Wallensak reel-to-reel tape recorder and a copy of the complete Robert Johnson outtakes that I had made for him. At that point, only one vinyl LP of Johnson's work had been

Many of the alternate takes were similar to the LP, but some were quite different. For example, the LP version of "Come On in My Kitchen" was soft and soothing with Johnson purring forth an enticing invitation to a woman. But the alternate version had a bold and strident sound with an aggressive and demanding Johnson.

Eric had never heard such powerful music before. He played along on an acoustic guitar, rewinding the tape to hear Johnson's technique over and over. It was near dawn when I packed up the tape recorder and headed home. I gave Eric the complete Johnson recordings and he was thrilled to get it.

As the years went by, I often read of various English guitar kings who had cut their blues teeth on the Robert Johnson tapes. They in-

ERIC
CLAPTON

released. I, on the other hand, had a copy of all the alternate takes that someone had smuggled out of the Columbia Records vault in Bridgeport, Connecticut.

We played the tape for hours, rewinding it to hear each song a second time.

nocently said, "I got it from Eric Clapton and he said that he got it from some guy in Boston."

Well, it has been almost four decades and he has always kept the secret secure.

He got it from me.

Opposite

DUSTER BENNETT, BUDDY GUY, ERIC CLAPTON, LONDON, 1969

A few years after that show in Boston, in the fall of 1967, I was in New York City with Skip James and Son House. Cream was also in town, so I called Eric at his hotel room. I told him that Skip and Son were with me and that we were leaving in the evening to begin a European tour. Eric and I agreed to meet at the Vanguard Records office.

The reception area was tiny, perhaps no more that fifteen feet by fifteen feet. A woman sat behind a telephone console, repeating over and over again, "Vanguard Records, how may I direct your call?" Skip, Son, and I sat in the three chairs facing the elevator and waited for Eric.

The door opened and Eric, expecting to step into a large reception area, took a long step forward and…froze. He was just a few feet away from two of his greatest heroes, the legends of the Delta blues that he loved so much.

I stood up and made the introductions. "Eric, this is Son House. Son, this is Eric Clapton who plays for a well-known English band." I continued, "Eric, this is Skip James. Skip, Eric is in the band that recorded your song, 'I'm So Glad.'"

I motioned for Eric to take my seat and they talked for a few minutes. Then Skip, never one to miss an opportunity at one-upmanship, took out his guitar and played "I'm So Glad" for Eric. The guitar then went to Son who, downing a sizable shot of bourbon first, played a riveting and deeply emotional song for his audience of three. Once he finished, Son offered the guitar to Eric and asked if he would play a song. Eric politely refused the offer.

Over the years, I've seen Eric a few times, but I've never mentioned that meeting at Vanguard. I wonder if he ever thinks back to that day when he took a long stride off the elevator and found himself face to face with two living legends.

Opposite

ERIC CLAPTON, LONDON, 1969

Ann Arbor, 1969

"**H**onesty" and "integrity" are *not weighty words in the* music industry. Some people stretch to attain minimal standards of decency, while others maintain high ones simply by their nature. In my years as a manager, Junior Wells was the benchmark by which all others were measured.

By an odd occurrence, I was his manager and booking agent before I ever met him. I had been working with traditional artists, all of them in their sixties or older. I knew that I was going to have to get some younger musicians or I wasn't going to be working for very long.

Bob Koester of Delmark Records told me that there was a whole generation of Chicago blues musicians just busting to get out of town and show their stuff. "Muddy and Wolf are touring, but there's a dozen others making great 45s for local companies and you ought to start working with some of these younger guys."

"O.K." I said, "Find me one who is talented, hard working, motivated, and ready to go out on tour."

Bob had just put the finishing touches on an album entitled *Hoodoo Man* by Junior Wells. It was the perfect fit for what I wanted. Bob made the call to Junior, who agreed to come out on the road and play some engagements that I would book for him.

I put together a few dates for him, starting with the 1966 Philadelphia Folk Festival and then continuing on to New York City, Cambridge, and a few other cities. For the first date, I drove down to a Philadelphia suburb called Paoli, where the festival was being held, and went onto the grounds looking for my new client. I found Junior sitting alone in the backstage tent and introduced myself. I showed him the set of contracts and discussed some payment details. Then I brought up the subject of whether he wanted to have a signed contract with me.

Junior took the cigarette out of his mouth and looked at me. "Koester says you're a righteous dude."

I nodded my head. "Well, I can do it either way. It's up to you."

He stood up and extended his hand to me. I got up and we shook hands.

"I don't need no paper," he said. "You make a dollar for me and I'll make a dollar for you."

I continued to manage Junior into the 1980s. We parted as friends and would continue to greet each other warmly at festivals. On those occasions, we often spent time talking and catching up on old friends.

In the mid-1990s, I sued a book for libel because they had used the phrase, "Waterman was roundly accused of being a thief." In a deposition, the author stated he had never directly heard that I was a thief, nor did he believe it to be true. He was also told that a Chicago blues musician had offered to "take care" of me. Under oath, he said that musician was Junior Wells.

Soon after the deposition, I was going to the San Francisco Blues Festival, which would give me an opportunity to let the scene play itself out in front of Junior directly. I went into the backstage tent, greeted him warmly, and then we sat down to talk. Junior was wearing a wide-brimmed white hat and he had his head down so that I could not see his face.

JUNIOR WELLS

🐾 *Above*

BUDDY GUY AND JUNIOR WELLS, ANN ARBOR, 1969

I told him about my libel suit against a book that accused me of being a thief. Furthermore, the author had stated that Junior was going to "take care" of me if I caused any problems. I paused and waited for Junior's reaction.

Cigarette smoke wafted upwards from around his hat brim and Junior slowly raised his head and looked at me. He eyes were like tiny dots of shotgun pellets, dark and riveting.

He reached forward and tapped my knee. "You tell me where to go to court and when to be there," he said softly.

I nodded my head and looked down at his hand on my knee.

He repeated it slowly. "You tell me where to be and when I got to be there. I'll set that motherfucker straight."

*J*unior Wells and I once played a memorable practical joke on Buddy Guy. Junior and Buddy were playing at The Riverboat in Toronto. Junior told me that someone had a leather coat to sell him but he was short on cash and needed a hundred dollars to pay for it. He would pay me back

Above
Buddy Guy and Junior Wells, Ann Arbor, 1969

at the end of the evening when the musicians got paid. In those days, I carried a hundred dollar bill folded up in my wallet. I took it out and put it in my shirt pocket in case Junior needed it.

A few moments later, I was sitting and talking to Buddy when Junior walked down the aisle of the club carrying the leather jacket. I reached into my pocket, held the hundred dollar bill up, and Junior took it from my hand without a word and kept on walking.

Buddy blinked and looked at me. "What the hell was that?"

I looked at him with a straight face.

"What was what?"

"Junior just come by and you give him a hundred dollar bill."

I leaned forward and looked at him seriously. "Why would I give Junior a hundred dollar bill? I work too hard for my money. You must have imagined it."

Agitated, Buddy pointed his finger at me and said, "Now don't you be fuckin' with me. You give Junior a goddamn hundred dollar bill and don't be telling me that I didn't see it!"

Junior and I kept the joke running for months until we finally confessed the truth to Buddy. Instead of being angry,

Above
BUDDY GUY AND JUNIOR WELLS, ANN ARBOR, 1969

Buddy turned it into his own joke. Whenever I would walk into a club where he was playing, Buddy would turn toward me and call out,

"Hey, Dick Waterman, give me a hundred dollar bill!"

<hr>

*Any honest photographer—any really honest photographer—*will tell you that the key to success is not the camera, the lens, or the film.

It is access.

I have been fortunate to have started my career in the music industry when the artist and photographer did not have an adversarial relationship; in a time when the backstage area might have been designated by a string or a line of chalk on the grass. Artists today feel that their image is a commercial entity to be protected and safeguarded.

We are now living in the world of the chic, the trendy, the "hotties,"—glittery icons of youth who are famous only to their mirrors. Access to today's artists is controlled by media people who are themselves only in their twenties.

Thank you, Lord, for letting me get in and out before I had to contend with all of that.

In 1970, when Buddy Guy and Junior Wells opened for the Rolling Stones on a lengthy European tour, we wore "ALL ACCESS" passes and simply disappeared into the background as the days passed. We were around the Stones day and night, in the airports and in the backstage areas. I wore a camera most of the time and it gave me incredible access to take photographs not available to others.

After Buddy and Junior did their show in Frankfurt, Mick Jagger came into the dressing room and started to talk to Junior about a certain harmonica technique. First, Mick played for Junior, who listened carefully. Then, Junior pointed to his head and told Mick that the blues sound Mick was looking for was something he had to feel in his mind. It wasn't just a matter if playing the instrument. He had to understand what the blues experience was all about and then bring it forth on his own. I snapped a series of pictures as they spoke and played for each other.

This type of photography is all about access.

Opposite
Junior Wells and Little Milton, San Francisco Blues Festival, 1995

Following
Mick Jagger Harmonica Lesson, Frankfurt, Germany, 1970

Above

Roosevelt Sykes and Big Mama Thornton, Ann Arbor, 1970

R O O S E V E L T

Roosevelt Sykes was definitely the sharpest dresser with whom I ever worked.

Times are different now (Allan Toussaint wears shades of brown and tan to match his Rolls Royce). But back then, Sykes was a man who took the time to get his ensemble together before he hit the streets. He favored three-piece suits with a gold watch on a chain running across his vest. He wore silk neckties, polished brogue shoes, and a homburg hat. Sykes was the last man I ever saw wear spats. He finished off his look with a gold handled walking stick that he carefully laid across the top of the piano before he sat down to play.

Sykes was a brilliant piano player and his influence can be heard in the technique of musicians like Toussaint, Art Neville, Doctor John, James Booker, and countless other New Orleans keyboard giants. He was also a sly old man who loved to slip a double entendre past an audience. My favorite was his lament, "If You See Kay," which was, of course, just his own way of slipping four letters of the alphabet past you.

S Y K E S

Boston, 1972

S ome people are tough to work with. *Others are extremely difficult* by nature. A very few are so miserable that the mere mention of their names brings horrific memories.

And then there is Big Mama Thornton.

It wasn't just that she was strong willed. I figured that she came out of the womb standing up and pissed off, and it just got worse from there. I had heard all of the usual horror stories about her and even watched her perform at a few festivals in the 1960s. By the early 1970s, I was booking a club called Joe's Place in Cambridge, and I brought her in for a week. Big Mama arrived with George "Harmonica" Smith to accompany her. To back her up, I hired a local band that I felt could really play her material and cover whatever weird changes she might pull on them. The place was packed on her opening night and things were moving along just fine when about 20 minutes in, she signaled the band to stop playing. My life got a lot worse right at that point.

Big Mama began to speak slowly, "Now when they hired me to come play here, they told me they'd have a band that could play my music. Well, you people is putting good money down to hear Big Mama play her best and I got to tell you that you ain't getting it. Now I got me a band back in Los Angeles that I wanted to bring with me but Dick Waterman…"

She stopped and looked out into the crowd. "*Whar* Dick Waterman?" she shouted.

I was trapped in the back of the crowd so I meekly raised my hand until she spotted me.

"*Thar* Dick Waterman!" she shouted. "Now Dick Waterman told me he had some band boys what knew my songs but I got to tell you that these boys are trying hard but they just can't cut it like my own band."

The band, furious at being humiliated in their own home town, stood motionless behind her. At the end of the evening, I stormed into the dressing room and announced, "OK, full rehearsal tomorrow at four o'clock. I can't have this mess going on all week."

Big Mama turned to me and shook her head. "What you talkin' about? These boys is *fine*. They didn't miss a change all night. I was having a little fun with them but these boys can flat out play!"

OK, OK, I thought. We were not communicating but we're all on the same page now. We got that little problem out of the way and the rest of the week will be fine.

The next night, she got about 20 minutes into the set and stopped the band again.

"Now I know you folks paid good money to hear Big Mama play her best. Now these boys is trying hard but they just ain't up to my band back in California. Now this band come to me because Dick Waterman said they could play my songs."

She paused and looked out over the crowd. "*Whar* Dick Waterman?"

I stood in the back of the crowd and shook my head. I realized that this miserable woman was going to do this to me every night of the

week's engagement. She had singled me out for her own private punishment and made my life a living hell.

However, an even worse fate was given to Jeffrey Hersh, my office manager and one of the sweetest individuals who ever made the wrong turn into the blues business. When Big Mama arrived in town, Jeffrey gave her his home number and told her to call him if she had any problems.

She called him at 1 a.m. every night. "Hey, you! I'm going to bed now."

Then she would call again every morning at 6 a.m. "Hey, you! I'm up now."

We put her up at the Suisse Chalet on the Arlington and Cambridge town lines. It wasn't fancy, but it was quite nice and I had booked many bands to stay there. Her first morning there, I had an urgent call from the hotel manager.

"You put this Thornton woman with us? You had better get out here right away."

I drove out to the Suisse Chalet and went into the building where Big Mama was staying. As I walked through the door, I was nearly overcome by a powerful, wretched stench. People were standing outside their doors with wet washcloths over their faces. I walked down the hall to Big Mama's room. There was no doubt where the smell was coming from. I knocked and waited to see what calamity was awaiting me on the other side of the door. She opened the door and the only thing that comes to mind is a Richard Pryor routine where he says, "The funk… come rushing out the door."

Choked with nausea, I walked in to find that she had a huge kettle cooking on a hot plate in the middle of the room. She lifted the lid and leaned in to savor the aroma.

"Ain't nothing like chitterlings and hog maws cooking in the morning," she announced.

I staggered out the door, raced down to hall and went into the parking lot to gasp fresh air. Having spent years managing them, I knew musicians who were obstinate, stubborn, difficult, and downright ornery.

Big Mama Thornton was in a league of her own.

Opposite
BIG MAMA THORNTON, BOSTON, 1972

Newport Folk Festival, 1968

I *was standing in the photographer's pit at the 1967 Newport Folk Festival* when I spotted John Cooke. I knew John as a member of the Charles River Valley Boys as well as a pretty good photographer. John had just come from the Monterey Pop Festival where he claimed to have witnessed a performance by the greatest talent ever. He became excited and joyous as he talked about her. "Her name is Janis Joplin and she is going to be a superstar. She's incredible. She just blew me away."

I respected John's opinion and made a mental note to find out more about Janis Joplin. All I knew was that she was a white blues rock singer from the Bay Area. Exactly one year later Janis was performing at the 1968 Newport Folk Festival, and I had an up-close view of what John had been describing.

She came on stage wearing a short velvet cape in spite of the sweltering July heat. After the first song, the cape was off and she was sweating profusely, working right at the front of the stage. Over the past 35 years, I have often said, "Working in the photo pit right in front of Janis Joplin was like putting your head down next to the rails when the express train passed."

Many icons of the music world died while their talents were still burning magnificently. Many left behind an important musical legacy. Think of Otis Redding, Brian Jones, Sam Cooke, Jimi Hendrix, Jim Morrison, Cass Elliott, and Jackie Wilson, for example. Yet, somehow, Janis is the least served by the passing of the years. Maybe it was because she didn't always sing on pitch or perhaps because she was a fashion disaster. Maybe it is simply because the video and recording equipment of the time were not capable of capturing her transcendent charisma.

In performance, Janis was completely into the song, the moment, the very instant of total abandonment into the music. She succeeded because she was not afraid to fail. Holding back nothing, Janis was entirely committed to a wild freefall of energy that left her totally exhausted.

When she finished a show, she would slump into a chair and put her head down. She had left everything behind her on stage.

Offstage, I knew Janis casually from spending some time with her in dressing rooms. Unlike the image she created of the tough whore with a heart of gold or the trash talking strong woman who would melt for the right guy, I found Janis to be bright and funny with a wide range of interests outside of the music business. She loved talking about movies and cooking. She told great Bill Graham stories.

I was on tour in Europe with Buddy Guy and Junior Wells, when I heard the news of her death on an English language station in Germany.

The public had forced her to live within a prison of her own creation. But now she was free to fly on her own.

I *once visited a small club on Divisidero Street in San Francisco to hear Big Mama Thornton. She was working through her second set*

when Janis and a male companion walked into the club and took a table right in front of the stage. Most of the small audience recognized her as she came in, but they looked away and gave her privacy.

Big Mama glanced down and saw Janis. She took the microphone off the stand and declared open season on her target.

"Well, now, some folks work hard and write songs and ain't got but nothing to show for it.

"But now some other people, they don't write no songs at all and they got themselves big fancy homes up in the hills.

"Now I wrote me a song called 'Ball and Chain' and I ain't seen no money—no money—comin' to me from my song. But now some people what done that song, they livin' high and they singin' about gettin' themselves a Mercedes Benz.

"It don't seem right that the person what wrote the song ain't seen no kind of money."

At that point, Janis had heard enough. She took a twenty dollar bill out of her purse, dropped it on the table, and she and her companion walked out of the club.

Previous

JANIS JOPLIN, NEWPORT FOLK FESTIVAL, 1968

Above

JANIS JOPLIN, NEWPORT FOLK FESTIVAL, 1968

Opposite

JANIS JOPLIN, NEWPORT FOLK FESTIVAL, 1968

Cambridge, 1972

J O S E P H

While working with the Boston Blues Society, I brought Joseph Spence up from Nassau to play a concert in Cambridge. I have not known many Bahamians in my life, but Joseph was one of the strangest individuals that I have ever met.

Joseph was the most self-centered person that I have ever encountered. Totally insensitive to others, he could be just plain dangerous around people with civility and manners. For instance, he might be eating dinner with three other people and there would be four pieces of chicken on the plate. The first two people would each take a piece and pass the plate along to Joseph. If Joseph was hungry, he would take the two remaining pieces and put the empty platter down on the table. There was also a time when I owned a two-door Pontiac LeMans. Whenever Joseph sat in the passenger seat, he would get out of the car and slam the door on the head of the person trying to get out from the back seat.

I once booked Joseph to play a concert with Mance Lipscomb at a small New Hampshire college. While driving there, we stopped at a Howard Johnson's to eat and I read the menu to them. They shook their heads at the mention of hamburger, cheeseburger, hot dog, and the other choices until I said "fish sandwich." They both brightened at that suggestion, so I ordered fish sandwiches all around.

Joseph was sitting on one side of the booth with Mance and me on the other side. A group of women were in the booth behind me, including one woman with a huge mane of thick blonde hair. The waitress brought the sandwiches and Joseph took a big bite of his. After a split second of hesitation, Joseph suddenly spat a mouthful of fish straight ahead, hitting Mance and me in the face and embedding a fat wad of chewed sandwich in the hair of the woman behind me.

He held the sandwich aloft. "Dis fiss?" he questioned.

I shrugged and nodded my head, dislodging pieces of the sandwich down into my lap. "That's what it says, Joseph. It's a fish sandwich."

He shook his head gravely and loudly announced, "Dis no fiss come fumdy sea."

S P E N C E

Boston, 1974

S I P P I E

*W*hile touring Europe in the mid-1960s, Sippie Wallace recorded an album for Storyville, a Swedish label. In the summer of 1968, Bonnie Raitt was traveling through Europe and stopped in London, where she found the album at Dobell's Record Store in the West End. Bonnie's career as a folk singer was just starting to get off the ground, and she added several of Sippie's songs to her repertoire. By the time she got her first contract with Warner Brothers in 1971, she was a devoted fan of Sippie Wallace.

What made Sippie unique was that she was one of the first female blues singers to write her own material. Most of the better known female vocalists from her era merely sang lyrics that had been written for them by men. Sippie, however, had her own outlook on a woman's role and was more than ready to put her thoughts into songs.

When Bonnie was booked into the 1972 Ann Arbor Blues & Jazz Festival, I reminded her that Sippie lived in nearby Detroit and set about to arrange a meeting. I contacted a young man named Ron Harwood who was looking after Sippie's career, such as it was. Ron worked

Sippie was in a wheelchair when she met Bonnie and announced that she had given up blues music to devote herself to the church. She rolled up close to the piano where David Maxwell, Bonnie's keyboard player, was playing one of Sippie's old songs. She listened intently and then began to tap her fingers and move her hand until, finally, she was waving her arm to guide him.

"Well, now, I don't sing blues no more but this is sounding so good that I might just take myself a little piece of it."

That was all that Bonnie needed to hear. They began quickly working out the arrangement for a duet. A few hours later, these two women who had never met were singing Sippie's songs together in front of 15,000 ecstatic fans.

As Bonnie's popularity grew throughout the 1970s, she incorporated Sippie into her show as the opening act. Bonnie often added Roosevelt Sykes to the bill because he had accompanied Sippie in the past. Despite the years of obscurity, Sippie was never shy or reserved on stage. She would bask in the applause, wave to the huge crowds, and ask over and over again, "How'm I doing? How'm I doing?"

W A Ł Ł A C E

tirelessly to promote her music and remind people that she was still alive and capable of performing. He brought Sippie to Ann Arbor, where she and Bonnie met for the first time. Sippie was brassy and straightforward. Bonnie has never been a shy, demure type, so the two of them immediately bonded into a friendship that would last for over 15 years.

In the years following their meeting in Ann Arbor, some of Bonnie's greatest performance moments took place on stage, joining in the applause of fans who were introduced to Sippie's music for the first time. Whatever Bonnie might have expected when she bought that Sippie Wallace album in London in 1968, I think the musical experience turned out to be better than she had ever dreamed.

Above
SIPPIE WALLACE AND BONNIE RAITT, BOSTON. 1974

Glendale, CA, 1991

C H A M P I O N

Champion Jack Dupree was the reason I came back to photography after not having picked up a camera for over 20 years. Taking pictures had never been an important part of my life, though I had been taking them casually until about 1970. Then I just got busy with other things, particularly when Bonnie Raitt decided to pursue a career in music, and Buddy Guy and Junior Wells were successful after opening for the Rolling Stones. In addition, I was booking the Chicago bands of Luther Allison and J.B. Hutto, as well as managing the solo careers of Son House, Fred McDowell, and Arthur "Big Boy" Crudup, among others.

I saw Champion Jack Dupree at the 1990 New Orleans Jazz & Heritage Festival. Promoter Quint Davis had flown Jack in from Germany just for that appearance. Jack also recorded for Rounder Records while he was in the U.S. I spoke to him briefly backstage and gave him my business card. I told him that if he ever wanted to come back for a longer tour, I would come out of retirement and be his agent. Jack eventually did call.

Champion Jack Dupree was the most focused person I ever met. He lived completely in the present moment, feeling that the past was irretrievably gone and the future still lay ahead. He had absolutely no sense of nostalgia or wish to reconnect with the past. Once I tried to talk to him about Fats Waller, James P. Johnson, and other legendary piano players. He turned his head and spat on the floor. "Fuck' em. They're dead. They ain't

here and I got a gig tonight. That's all I'm thinking about."

On the night Jack played Wolf Trap in Vienna, Virginia, my mother had a major stroke following routine surgery. The hospital called and told me to rush home because she was not going to survive for very long. I dropped Jack and guitarist Ken Lending in Woodstock, and headed straight for my hometown of Plymouth, Massachusetts. I was just at the state line between Connecticut and Massachusetts when a state trooper pulled me over for speeding. I sat in the car and watched in the rear view mirror as he got out of his car and walked towards me. I looked at my reflection in the mirror and talked to myself.

"Officer, I'm rushing to the bedside of my dying mother."

I tried it again.

"Officer, I know you won't believe this but I am rushing to the bedside of my dying mother." I shook my head and knew that I couldn't sell that line. I let him write me up and then I headed on my way.

My mother passed away shortly after I got there. I stayed overnight and then rushed back to take Jack and Ken from Woodstock up to their engagement in Rochester. I then got a flight back to Boston and drove home for my mother's funeral. The following day, I flew to Canada to meet them and resume the tour.

Several weeks later, I was driving with Jack sitting next to me and Ken napping in the back seat. Jack chewed on the butt of his cigar and said quietly, "I didn't tell you I was

J A C K   D U P R E E

sorry your mother died."

I nodded my head and said, "Thank you, Jack, I appreciate that."

He turned his head and said, "I didn't tell you that I was sorry that your mother died. I said, I didn't tell you that I was sorry that your mother died."

Well, I figured that he had something to say and he was going to do it in his own way so I just kept my eyes on the road.

He took the cigar out of his mouth and studied it for a few seconds and then turned towards me, "Now in order for me to tell you that I was sorry that you lost your mother, I would have had to have known what it was like to have a mother.

"Now since I never knew what it was like to have a mother, then I never knew what it was like to lose a mother. But...if I had known what it was like to have a mother...and I knew what it was like to lose a mother...then I could tell you that I was sorry that you lost your mother."

I waited a few seconds and then turned my head towards him. "Thank you, Jack."

He nodded his head and put the cigar back in his mouth.

⌐ Previous

CHAMPION JACK DUPREE, GLENDALE, CA, 1971

Opposite ▷

CHAMPION JACK DUPREE, GLENDALE, CA, 1991

Glendale, CA, 1991

Willie Dixon is one of the very few blues artists who actually became prosperous during his lifetime. Originally from Vicksburg, Mississippi, Willie was a big man who was also a pretty good boxer, winning the Illinois Golden Gloves heavyweight championship shortly after he moved to Chicago.

Willie wrote hit songs for Muddy Waters, Howling Wolf, and Koko Taylor, but the real money started to come in the 1960s when English groups such as the Rolling Stones, Animals, Yardbirds, and others had major hits with his songs. A savvy businessman, Willie understood the arcane world of publishing, sub-publishing, and the foreign licensing of his material. He could turn a single recording session into multiple sources of income by bringing to his home studio a rhythm section, a guitarist, a piano player, and a harmonica player, all of whom sang. They would work all day and night with each musician taking turns as the vocalist, recording enough material for a whole album. Willie would mix and master the recordings on his own and then license each of them individually to companies in England, France, Germany, and other countries hungry for good Chicago blues.

After he had leased the recordings of individual artists, Willie would create compilation albums and start licensing them all over again. Of course, he had written all of the songs and held all of the publishing rights as well. Once he got rich, he was very generous with his success and formed The Blues Heaven Foundation in 1982 which provided inner city children with musical instruments.

In the spring of 1991 while travelling with Champion Jack Dupree, I visited Willie at his modest home in Glendale, just outside of Los Angeles. Marie Dixon cooked a delicious chicken lunch for us and afterward Willie took Jack and me to a bungalow that he had behind his house. It was completely jammed with sheet music, albums, CDs, trophies, award plaques, and the memorabilia of a half-century in music.

Willie was still actively involved in an amazing number of projects throughout the 1990s. He was about to record some young musicians from East Los Angeles and fuse Chicago blues with their Latino rhythms when I saw him. He had a meeting scheduled with director Oliver Stone about doing a soundtrack for a film, and was busy putting together new compilations of some of his older hits.

Willie didn't rest on past successes. He was always pushing himself forward and he stayed busy right up until he died.

WILLIE DIXON

Opposite
Willie Dixon, Glendale, CA, 1991

Austin, TX, 1993

In 1993, I was in Austin photographing Willie Nelson's 60th birthday party. A stunning list of talent had been assembled for the celebration: Waylon Jennings, Paul Simon, Bonnie Raitt, B. B. King, Lyle Lovett, Emmylou Harris, and so many others. But if there is a "first among equals" in the world of the exceptionally talented, it must be a position reserved for Ray Charles. When he comes to the stage, even artists who are superstars themselves stop what they are doing and turn to watch.

This photograph was actually brought into being by Candace Spearman, my Memphis darkroom technician who makes miracles

RAY

CHARLES

happen on a routine basis. The original negative shows the outline of the state of Texas on the back wall as well as the visible outline of the entire band including Don Was on bass and Mickey Raphael on harmonica. Candace suggested that if I let her burn the negative longer everything would vanish except the singular spotlight shining down on Ray.

I gave her the go-ahead to take a shot at it and the result is a photograph that immediately catches people's attention as they look at a musician basking in the glory of audience appreciation.

It is my negative, but it is Candace's photograph.

Ray Charles, New Orleans, 1995

Opposite
Ray Charles, Austin, 1993

Mississippi, 1993

A L B E R T

C O L L I N S

I didn't know Albert Collins very well. I met him a few times and he was always friendly enough.

On the final night of the 1993 Mississippi Valley Blues Festival, I was taking the film out of my cameras when I noticed that one camera still had a few negatives to be used. Since I had to go past the main stage on my way to the parking lot, I walked over to where Albert was performing. The stage was about chest high so I leaned onto the apron and raised my camera. I clicked off several shots, but I knew that I wasn't getting anything good. Albert was behind the microphone stand, blocked from my view.

I was down to my final shot when I glanced up and saw Albert looking straight at me. He nodded his head once, took one step to his left, and squared off to face me. He was looking right down the lens of the camera. I squeezed off the last shot in the roll and nodded my thanks to him as he went back behind the microphone. As I look at that shot now, I can see that Albert is riddled with the cancer that would take his life in just a few months.

It's the only good shot I ever got of Albert and it came to me as a personal gift.

Opposite

ALBERT COLLINS, DAVEPORT, IOWA, 1993

Santa Cruz, CA, 1996

C H A R L E S

*C*harles Brown was a man who found optimism in the depths of a miserable world. He would tell you that the glass was half-full when you couldn't even find the glass. He was probably the most positive thinking man that I had ever met. It didn't matter how much bad fortune came upon him. He believed that every day, every hour, every minute was worth living to the fullest.

Although he never attained wide commercial popularity, his talent was far-reaching. Ray Charles has often said that Charles Brown was his biggest influence, both as a piano player and as a vocalist. Charles was a college graduate and taught science for many years before committing himself to a career in music. In 1947, with the hit "Merry Christmas, Baby," he found seasonal work every Decem-ber. By the 1960s, hard times had set in. It would be twenty years before Bonnie Raitt discovered the talents of Charles. She worked hard to get him a recording contract and featured him on a number of lengthy tours.

This photograph of Charles wasn't planned. I was at the 1996 Santa Cruz Blues Festival and had just put a new roll of film in my camera. I always waste the first negative since it is usually exposed to light when loaded into the camera. I had just put the roll in when I looked up and saw Charles coming around the corner from the backstage area. I raised the camera and hit the shutter at the same time. It came as an accident, but the result is a genuine "keeper." It captures the wonderful smile of a man who suffered through bad times, but managed to find sheer joy in everything that he did.

BROWN

Clarksdale, 1996

JUNIOR

There are several variations of Mississippi blues and the best known is the Delta style of Son House, Robert Johnson, and Muddy Waters. But farther northeast you'll find the "hill country" music of Fred McDowell, R. L. Burnside, and Junior Kimbrough.

After his appearance in the 1991 documentary *Deep Blues*, Junior enjoyed a measure of success in his final years. He released several Fat Possum recordings, including his critically acclaimed album, *All Night Long*, as well as *Sad Days, Lonely Nights* and *Most Things Haven't Worked Out.*

He also owned Junior's Place, a juke joint in Holly Springs, Mississippi. There was live music at Junior's Place only on Sunday nights, but you never knew which Sunday. Junior's was about a forty-five minute drive from either Memphis or Oxford, and he simply refused to put in a telephone. Driving out to his place was a crapshoot. If Junior felt like being open, he came down the road from his house and opened up. If he didn't feel like being open, he didn't. Simple as that.

However, nearby Oxford, home to University of Mississippi, often hosted large contingents of tourists from many countries. People were eager to see and hear "real deal" music, and Junior's Place was about as rustic and primitive as you could find. Many a busload of tourists and university students made the trek to Junior's only to discover that he had simply decided not to be open that night. In 2000, two years after his death, Junior's Place burned down.

KIMBROUGH

Opposite

Junior Kimbrough, Clarksdale, 1996

You think that you really know *Bobby Rush*. He's the electrifying charismatic soul blues singer that lights up an audience with his incandescent show featuring double entendres and pneumatic dancing from his "hootchie girls."

You don't know him at all.

Bobby Rush is not even the type of guy who always has that wicked, leering grin while holding up a gigantic pair of panties and extolling the virtues of a "big fat mama."

Wrong again.

The real Bobby Rush is a soft-spoken guy who will take his band anywhere, at any time, to play a benefit, help a charity or do a free show for someone who helped him out years earlier. Bobby is the one who goes to the hospitals in Jackson, Mississippi, to play harmonica and entertain the children who don't get many visitors. There are no "hootchie girls" in tow—he's just a guy spending some time with sick children.

In 2001, Bobby's tour bus was in a major accident with one band member killed and many others badly injured. But two weeks later he was performing, hobbling to the edge of the stage on crutches and waiting for his introduction at a special concert. Once he heard his name, he dropped the crutches and went on stage to play a magnificent set of typical Bobby Rush material—naughty, raunchy, and a whole lot of fun.

When he finished, he made his way to the side of the stage and sat down to rest for a minute before reaching for the crutches again.

Was he there for a big pay night?

No. Bobby was just fulfilling a request to play a benefit concert that he had promised to do long before the bus accident.

Bobby gave one of the eulogies at the funeral of the long-time Clarksdale radio personality Early Wright. It was more of a celebration of Early's life than an occasion for solemn mourning.

Bobby told the story of a time when he was feeling depressed that his career was not going well. He decided to try a different musical direction, so he worked up some new material and took it to a radio station in Birmingham. According to Bobby, the people at the radio station didn't like the record and told him that he sounded "too black." He brought the record over to Early Wright and played it for him. Bobby asked Early if he sounded "too black."

Early looked at him for a long time and then shook his head slowly. "Well, now seeing as how I'm looking at you standing right in front of me, I don't see how they could have called it any other way!"

Opposite

Bobby Rush at the King Biscuit Blues Festival, Helena, AR, 1996

M

A few years ago, I made a short list of the living artists I hadn't photographed and still wanted to. I decided to make a serious effort to find out where they were playing and use my saved airline mileage to go after them. At the top of the list was Pops Staples. Originally from Drew, Mississippi, Pops was the scion of one of the finest gospel groups, the Grammy-nominated Staples Singers. The four Staples children sang alongside their father, Pop Staples, who accompanied them on guitar.

They were performing at the 1997 Bull Durham Blues Festival in North Carolina, so I made a point of attending and shot quite a few pictures of him. But though the work was good, there were no images that I felt were exceptional. However, Mavis, the lead singer of the three daughters, stood out and was a joy to watch. Some women influence other female singers without realizing fame themselves. This is certainly true of Mavis Staples.

I came away with this photograph, not at all disappointed that I had not captured a compelling image of her father.

A V I S

S T A P L E S

Opposite

MAVIS STAPLES, DURHAM, NC. 1997

Cleveland, 1997

Let's say that everyone on earth is allocated a certain number of curse words to use in their lifetime. Now take a couple of thousand nuns and remove their curse words because they won't ever use them. Take the curse words and give them to a hot-tempered man in his late 80s with a bad attitude and a short fuse.

Welcome to the world of Robert Lockwood.

To put it quite simply, Robert has no tact, no civility, no sense of decorum, and a total inability not to give you the blunt truth right to your face. And I love him madly.

Lockwood's mother was briefly married to the great Robert Johnson back in the 1930s, so Robert Lockwood is often referred to as "Robert Junior Lockwood" or "Robert Lockwood Junior." Even though Robert Johnson has been dead for 65 years, people sometimes forget that Lockwood himself has made dozens of albums in a wide variety of blues and jazz stylings. He has worked solo, as part of a duo, with a blues band, with a jazz band with horns, and in just about every other blues incarnation, yet people feel that they have the right to simply walk up to him and start talking about Robert Johnson, completely ignoring Lockwood's own vast body of work assembled over the decades.

Lockwood lives in Cleveland, home of the Rock and Rock Hall of Fame and Museum. Once, when I was talking to a senior executive of the Hall, I reminded him that one of the blues legends lived in his very city, and perhaps the institution should pay him to play every Friday afternoon or invite him to teach a Master Class in blues guitar.

I saw Robert some months later and asked if anyone from the Hall had contacted him.

"Yeah, they come by the house," he said. "You know what they wanted? They wanted me to donate a guitar to them. Like I got so many motherfucking guitars that I can be giving them away."

One evening, Robert was playing at B.B.'s Lawnside Barbecue in Kansas City. Club owner Lindsey Shannon has developed an older clientele who come for the good food and to hear the music. As Robert began his first song, a man came walking down the aisle toward him with a camcorder, focusing on the musician as the cameraman came closer and closer. Robert, ever the cordial diplomat, stopped playing and stared at the man.

"Now just what the fuck you think you doing?"

The crowd gasped and women covered their mouths with their hands.

"You get that motherfucker out of my face or I ain't playing no show."

Lindsey came rushing out of the kitchen, corralled the man, and escorted him out of the club.

In the mid-1990s, Robert apparently heard about the libel suit against an author who accused me of being dishonest. He asked if it was true. Yes, I told him, I had been described as a crook in print. He asked me if I wanted him to appear in court on my behalf. I was surprised at this offer because I had never been his manager or booking agent, and we had few business dealings over the years. I nodded my head and told him that if I could get the case into a courtroom, he could be of great help to me.

Robert started to walk away and then turned back. "You are one of the ugliest motherfuckers that I have ever met but at least you're honest."

Shack, Mississippi delta

O
T
H
A
R

thar Turner was a farmer who lived in Gravel Springs, Mississippi, near Senatobia, a region known for their fife and drum corps. Othar Turner and the Rising Star Fife and Drum Band, which included a few family members, were part of a musical tradition that predates the blues. Since he first laid hands on a cane fife at the age of 16, Othar would go into the marshland, cut reeds, and make his own cane fifes. Many of the blues festivals in the South would traditionally open with Othar playing the fife and leading two snare players and a bass player. The foursome would enter the festival grounds and the crowd would follow.

Right up until his death in 2003, Othar hosted a very popular annual goat roast. Once people found out when and where the roast was taking place, they would come from all over the country. He would barbecue goat, drink bad liquor, and take out the cane fife, while everyone would sit around, eat, drink, and enjoy music deep into the night.

T U R N E R

Opposite

OTHAR TURNER, ROCK AND ROLL HALL OF FAME AND MUSEUM, 2000

St. Louis, 1996

Etta James may be one of the greatest female singers of all time. I put her up there with Bessie Smith and Aretha Franklin, but, Lord have mercy, if you look up the word "diva" in the dictionary, you'll find a picture of Etta as the illustration.

Once, I was promoting her at a small Berkeley club called Larry Blake's on Telegraph Avenue. Etta came into the club while the opening act was on and walked through the room waving at people. Smiling, shaking hands, and having a fine time, she went through the back door and into the dressing room. I went up to check on the box office when one of the club employees came running up the stairs to tell me that Etta went out the rear entrance of the club and was on her way back to her motel.

I raced downstairs and got on stage to announce that there would be a slightly longer intermission than usual, but that the great Etta James would come onstage shortly. I jumped in my car with the club manager and we drove like crazed banshees to her motel. We got to her room and knocked on the door. She was in there but she wasn't coming out.

"OK," I said, "what's the problem? Is it anything that a little money can cure?"

"No." Etta proceeds to tell us through the door that a vision she had with her "third eye" told her not to perform.

"Will some extra money make the 'third eye' see things a bit differently?"

"No." She wasn't coming out and that was final.

The club manager and I drove back to Larry Blake's. I told him that he had to go on stage and tell the crowd that Etta was not going to appear. "Tell them to be calm and that everybody will get their money back."

He gave me a look that said, "That club is full of Indians and my name is Tonto. That means that you get your Dick Waterman ass on stage and tell them that she is not appearing."

Back at the club, the crowd had been waiting for a long time and was getting very angry. The mood brightened as I ambled onstage and gave the crowd a little wave. They thought I was going to introduce Etta.

"Listen, we have a little problem," I began. "Etta James has taken sick and she isn't going to perform tonight."

A guy at the front table jumped to his feet. "What the fuck you talkin' about? She just come through here and shook my hand. What kind of asshole stunt are you pulling here?"

Suffice it to say that it got worse from there. I consider myself fortunate to have escaped physically intact, but emotionally battered and prohibited from ever promoting a show in Berkeley again.

In spite of it all, Etta is still a "diva"—an artist with a temperamental personality and unpredictable ways. She is vain to a turn, but she also has talent so profound that it transcends every problem and makes troublesome peccadilloes fall away. She has put on a lot of weight in recent years and that really makes it difficult for photographers. When I was shooting at the 1995 St. Louis Blues Festival, she came on stage and the first thing she did was to order the lighting man to kill the whites, the yellows, the pale blues, and the pinks. Etta stood at the back of the stage and leaned on a metal stool with only deep red and blue lights on her.

But when Etta James hits the first line of "At Last," I am ready to forgive her every fault and stand in line to promote her again.

Well, maybe not in Berkeley.

Above

ETTA JAMES, ST. LOUIS, 1996

Long Beach, CA, 1997

JOHN

I saw *John Lee Hooker at the 1997 Long Beach Blues Festival.* After taking some photographs of him from the front pit, I went around to the back steps leading onto the stage. I waited until John's manager, Mike Kappus, glanced down and saw me. He nodded his head and gave me the chance to come up and shoot from the back of the stage.

When John finished playing, the band continued the beat while he stood up and approached the front of the stage and waved his arm to the crowd. I shot furiously, hoping to get the exact image that I wanted to take away with me. As soon as the film was developed, I glanced at the negatives to make certain that they looked sharp and had good contrast. Then I put them in a drawer and waited for the time that I did not want ever to arrive.

When John died in 2001, I took the negatives out of the drawer and examined them closely to see if I could find the one I wanted to use. It shows John from the back, his oddly jointed right hand silhouetted against the sky.

Once and for all time, John Lee Hooker says goodbye.

LEE HOOKER

Opposite
JOHN LEE HOOKER, SANTA CRUZ, CA, 1996

ACKNOWLEDGMENTS

This is my first book after 40 years in the music business, and it would be impossible for me to acknowledge every musician, manager, agent, promoter or record company executive who has helped along the way.

However, I must name some individuals whose artistic vision combined with their personal values of ethics and integrity made an indelible mark upon me and provided guidance even as I floundered.

And so I offer my gratitude for the gift of friendship that I received from my mentors: Bill Graham, George Wein, Manny Greenhill and Jerry Wexler.

This book would not have been possible without the dedication and commitment of Chris Murray. He first saw my photographs in the window of a tiny framing store in Oxford, Mississippi, in 1996. They were poorly printed, carelessly matted and badly hung but Chris saw something in my work that sustained him for the seven years it took to bring forth this book.

I must acknowledge the work of other photographers with whom I have worked over the past four decades. As the first among equals, Ernest Withers and David Gahr make the footsteps in which we walk. I also salute the work of Jack Vartoogian, Baron Wolman, Jim Marshall, Bill Allard and Marc Norberg. As I continue to photograph, it is a joy to work with Jef Jaison and Chuck Winan.

I would like to thank Dick Garfield, my Cambridge roommate and fellow photographer. We shot dozens of rolls of film at Newport festivals and then returned home to stay up all night developing them two at a time on the floor of the bathroom. These negatives make up a significant part of this book, and I am indebted to him for his skill under primitive conditions.

If the measure of a man is the devotion of his friends, then I am truly blessed because of Alexandra and Peter Guralnick. They have provided encouragement, support and patience beyond measure as I often seemed incapable of bringing forth a book.

If this book is found to have any merit at all, then it shall stand as my enduring gratitude to them.

Opposite
JOHN LEE HOOKER, SAN FRANCISCO, 1995

Following
JOHN LEE HOOKER

DICK WATERMAN

ACKNOWLEDGMENTS

I am truly grateful for the support of several individuals on this project. To my son David Murray, who first suggested we trace the roots of the blues. To master printer David Adamson and his assistants, John Hughes and Wade Hornung, for invaluable work with Dick Waterman's archive. To my dear friend and fellow blues devotee Bill Paley, whose enthusiasm for Dick Waterman's photographs and the blues helped keep this project on track. To David Friend who recognized the vision for this book. To Scott Stuckey, for helping me document many of Dick Waterman's stories. To Candace Spearman, Carol Reed, Meredith Arthur, and Kathy Kane for their support. To Raoul Goff and Ian Szymkowiak for realizing a great design. To Bonnie Raitt for her dedication and love of the blues.

A most special thank you to Carol Huh, whose editorial assistance with this book was invaluable. Thank you, Carol, for pulling it all together...I am truly and forever grateful.

I can not thank enough Peter Guralnick for his contribution to this book. His deep appreciation and understanding of Dick Waterman's work helped me immeasurably. His encouragement meant everything to me. Thank you, Peter—words can not fully express my gratitude.

And most of all, a heartfelt thank you to Dick Waterman. Your photographs and stories pass to us all a legacy that goes to our very souls. You have taught me so much. Thank you, Dick, for being witness to the blues.

CHRIS MURRAY

COLOPHON

CBETWEEN MIDNIGHT & DAY
was produced by **Insight Editions**
for **Thunder's Mouth Press**
www.insighteditions.com

Chris Murray, *Senior Editor*

Raoul Goff, *Creative Director*

Gordon Goff, *Marketing*

Carol Huh, *Project Editor*

Ian Szymkowiak, *Design*

Usana Shadday, *Production Manager*

Alan Hebel, *Production Assistant*

Candace Spearman, *Production Prints*

Meredith Arthur, *Copy Editor*

Carol Reed, *Editor*

With special thanks to the staff at
Govinda Gallery

The text typeface is Baskerville and the
display faces are Eremaeus and Galleon.

The text stock is 140 gsm Japanese matte
art paper and printed four color with
spot gloss varnish.

This book was printed and
bound by
Palace Press International
Hong Kong, under the
supervision of
Raoul Goff and **Usana Shadd**

www.palacepress.com